Additional pra
Filial Therapy: Strengthe
Relationships Through F

D0558094

Dr. VanFleet's third edition of her Filial Therap
First for the Guerneys who developed this model and sougnt to empower parents by
giving them skill sets that produce positive change in the parent-child relationship;
and secondly, for Filial Therapy, one of the most effective approaches to relationship
enhancement. This edition asserts the credibility and applicability of this evidence- and
practice-informed model, and shows it has great potential to help with an array of con-
temporary challenges faced by children and their families. Dr. VanFleet has the kind of
passion and clarity that combine to create accessible and inspiring reading for novice
and veteran clinicians.

Eliana Gil, PhD
Founding Partner, Gil Institute for Trauma Recovery and Education, Fairfax, Virginia

In this handy and concise book, Rise VanFleet has made it easy for the novice as well
as experienced practitioners to grasp Filial Therapy and integrate this powerful and ef-
fective approach with children and families. This up-to-date edition includes a rich de-
scription of the theoretical approaches that have informed Filial Therapy and how they
are integrated. It has retained the essential features that clearly explain the values and
principles, methods, and applications of Filial Therapy. Given my more than 40 years
of clinical practice applying Filial Therapy, I am amazed at how much useful information
Dr. VanFleet has packed into this slim book.

Barry G. Ginsberg, PhD, Executive Director of The Center of Relationship
Enhancement (CORE); author of *Relationship Enhancement Family Therapy*
and *50 Wonderful Ways to Be a Single-Parent Family*

Dr. VanFleet has written a brilliant book that distills the essence of Filial Therapy. Her
writing is clear and practical, with step-by-step directions for teaching parents Filial
Therapy and case studies that illuminate the process. I especially like the way she has
included information on Filial Therapy research, alternative formats for Filial Therapy,
and application to special populations.

Terry Kottman, PhD, RPT-S, NCC, LMHC
Director, The Encouragement Zone, Cedar Falls, Iowa
Author of *Partners in Play: An Adlerian Approach to Play Therapy* and
Play Therapy: Basics and Beyond

Praise from the Second Edition of
Filial Therapy: Strengthening Parent-Child
Relationships Through Play

In the past decade a growing number of child therapists are incorporating Filial Therapy
in their practice. This timely Second Edition reflects the current 'state-of-the-art' of this
popular Play Therapy Intervention. Highly recommended!

Charles E. Schaefer, PhD, RPT-S, Director-Emeritus
Association for Play Therapy

A timely update due to the rapidly growing interest in Filial Therapy both in the United
States and across the world. Dr. VanFleet has made a wonderful book, which includes
the 'how-to' for conducting Filial Therapy, even more comprehensive by including the
research and applications of Filial Therapy, as well as the multicultural aspects of this
field. This book is a must for any clinician working with children and families.

Heidi G. Kaduson, PhD, RPT-S, Director, The Play Therapy Training
Institute, Inc.; Private practice, Monroe Township, NJ and New York, NY

Filial Therapy

Strengthening Parent-Child Relationships Through Play

Third Edition

Risë VanFleet

Professional Resource Press
Sarasota, FL

Published by
Professional Resource Press
(An imprint of Professional Resource Exchange, Inc.)
Post Office Box 3197 • Sarasota, FL 34230-3197
Printed in the United States of America
Copyright © 1994, 2005, 2014 by Professional Resource Exchange, Inc.

This publication is sold with the understanding that the publisher is not engaged in rendering professional services. If legal, psychological, medical, accounting, or other expert advice or assistance is sought or required, the reader should seek the services of a competent professional.

Library of Congress Cataloging-in-Publication Data

VanFleet, Risë, date.
  Filial therapy : strengthening parent-child relationships through play / Risë VanFleet.
-- Third edition.
      pages cm
  Includes bibliographical references.
  ISBN-13: 978-1-56887-145-5 (alk. paper)
  ISBN-10: 1-56887-145-7 (alk. paper)
  1. Play therapy. 2. Parent and child. I. Title.
  RJ505.P6V36 2013
  618.92'891653--dc23

                                                            2013016282

DEDICATION

This book is dedicated to my parents,
Robert and Frieda VanFleet,
with gratitude for the
warm, encouraging, and playful
family atmosphere they created for us.

ACKNOWLEDGMENTS

Many people have contributed to the initial creation of this monograph and the subsequent revised editions. I am especially grateful to Dr. Samuel Knapp, who first encouraged me to write this guide and who provided valuable input. I am also indebted to the many professionals who have read and provided feedback to me about this book during the last two decades. Professionals who have been using Filial Therapy in creative ways with many different families, and researchers who have continued to explore the processes and outcomes of this approach have contributed significantly to our understanding and use of Filial Therapy today.

I have continued to learn a great deal from the many children and families with whom I have worked. Our collaborative use of Filial Therapy has taught me much, and these families' experiences and input are represented substantially in the revisions.

I am indebted once again to publisher and editor Dr. Lawrence Ritt, managing editor Laurie Girsch, and all the staff of Professional Resource Press. As with the other editions, their friendly, supportive approach, helpful suggestions, and professionalism have made this process truly enjoyable.

I also thank my husband, Mark Zarichansky, for his patience and encouragement of this and related projects that consume my time and energy. I am particularly indebted to my parents, Robert and Frieda VanFleet, who have tirelessly supported my various interests and whose influence has helped me become a better therapist and a better writer.

Most of all, however, I am deeply grateful to Dr. Louise Guerney and Dr. Bernard Guerney, who pioneered Filial Therapy in the 1960s and have been developing it ever since. They have been wonderfully encouraging and caring teachers, innovators, and friends. Much of the material in this guide I first learned from them. As the years pass, my admiration of them and their work just grows and grows. Their vision and leadership continue to help countless families throughout the world.

SERIES PREFACE

As a publisher of books, multimedia materials, and continuing education programs, the Professional Resource Press strives to provide clinical and forensic professionals with highly applied resources that can be used to enhance skills and expand practical knowledge.

All of the titles in the Practitioner's Resource Series are designed to provide important new information on topics of vital concern to psychologists, clinical social workers, counselors, psychiatrists, and other clinical and forensic professionals.

Although the focus and content of each title in this series will be quite different, there will be notable similarities:

1. Each title in the series will address a timely topic of critical importance.

2. The target audience for each title will be practicing professionals. Our authors were chosen for their ability to provide concrete "how-to-do-it" guidance to colleagues who are trying to increase their competence in dealing with complex problems.

3. The information provided in these titles will represent "state-of-the-art" information and techniques derived from both experience and empirical research. Each of these guidebooks will include references and resources for those who wish to pursue more advanced study of the discussed topics.

4. The authors will provide case studies, specific recommendations, and the types of "nitty-gritty" details that practitioners need before they can incorporate new concepts and procedures into their offices.

We feel that one of the unique assets of Professional Resource Press is that all of our editorial decisions are made by practitioners.

The publisher, all editorial consultants, and all reviewers are practicing psychologists, marriage and family therapists, clinical social workers, and psychiatrists.

If there are other topics you would like to see addressed in this series, please let me know.

Lawrence G. Ritt, Publisher

FOREWORD

It is an honor to be asked to write the foreword for the third edition of Risë VanFleet's widely recognized *Filial Therapy* book. Dr. VanFleet is the leading U.S. figure in the education and publishing of the Guerney Model of Filial Therapy.

The author has expanded and enhanced what was already a wonderful previous edition. Outstanding is the revised section on "Theoretical Integration," in which she lays out the seven theoretical sources underlying the complex approach that is Filial Therapy. She also gives a clear explanation of the psychoeducational approach, of which Filial Therapy is one of the first. The many facets of Filial Therapy are made readily understandable. The author uses case examples to clarify points.

Reading this book would allow those who wish to pursue the method, or brush up on its finer points, to do so. Of course, additional training and supervision are highly recommended to become truly proficient.

Dr. VanFleet's focus is on Filial Therapy for individual families. In addition, she explains how to adapt the model for application with children and families with special clinical issues. She emphasizes the value of working with as many family members as possible – including siblings – to attain the best outcomes.

Experienced or new to Filial Therapy, a therapist will find many touches not found elsewhere. I can recommend this book without reservation to professionals seeking an efficient, effective method for working with families. Dr. VanFleet presents a convincing rationale, as well as detailed guidance on how to apply the model for therapeutic or preventive purposes, in clinical or educational settings. In this volume, of readable size, Dr. VanFleet packs in all the essential information the Filial Therapist will need.

Louise Guerney, PhD, RPT-S
Professor Emerita, The Pennsylvania State University
North Bethesda, MD

ABSTRACT

Filial Therapy has been shown through 50 years of research and clinical experience to be an effective intervention for children and families experiencing a variety of social, emotional, and behavioral difficulties. This unique therapy involves parents as the primary change agents to resolve child-related problems, to encourage children's healthy psychosocial development, and to strengthen entire families. Filial therapists train and supervise parents as the parents conduct child-centered play sessions with their children, an approach that not only helps eliminate presenting problems but also strengthens parent-child and family relationships. This guide covers the principles, theoretical foundations, research, concepts, and specific methods used in Filial Therapy. Common problems are discussed, and one family's experience is followed throughout the course of therapy.

In the 20 years since this volume was first published, public and professional interest in Filial Therapy has grown substantially throughout the world. Research on the approach continues to grow. The third edition elaborates on the principles, values, and theories on which Filial Therapy is based and updates the research as well as the applications of the method with a wide range of presenting problems. References have been updated, derivative formats have been included, and the method's multicultural value continues to be highlighted.

TABLE OF CONTENTS

Filial Therapy

Strengthening
Parent-Child Relationships
Through Play
(3rd Edition)

BACKGROUND

Countless articles in newspapers, popular magazines, and professional journals have reported disheartening stories and statistics about the problems facing children and families today. Our world is changing rapidly and dramatically, and some fear that society's basic unit, the family, may not survive the turmoil.

Although current trends seem grim, signs of strength and hope do exist. Strong families of many configurations remain, and we are learning more about what makes them strong (Stinnett & DeFrain, 1985). Parents seem more willing to attend parent education programs, and more families are seeking professional help to cope with their problems. Professionals may very well have greater opportunities to assist children and families with intervention and prevention efforts than ever before.

Filial Therapy can be an extremely useful tool in helping children and families overcome or prevent problems that might otherwise weaken them. Developed during the 1960s by Dr. Louise Guerney and Dr. Bernard Guerney as a treatment for children with social, emotional, and behavioral problems (B. G. Guerney, 1964; L. F. Guerney, 1976a, 1983a, 1991, 1997, 2000, 2003a, 2003b; L. F. Guerney & Ryan, 2013), Filial Therapy has received increasing recognition by the clinical and research communities as an effective approach to strengthening parent, child, and family relationships.

In Filial Therapy, parents become the primary change agents as they learn to conduct child-centered play sessions with their own children. Filial therapists, using a competence-oriented psychoeducational framework, teach parents to conduct specialized play sessions, supervise parents during these play sessions, and help them eventually integrate the play sessions and parenting skills at home.

Filial Therapy is most frequently used with children aged 3 to 10 or 12 years, but in some trauma cases, the use of Filial Therapy has been extended to children in their mid-teens with little alteration required.

The substitution of child-centered "special times" for the play sessions can easily extend its applicability to other adolescents as well. Special times involve activities selected by the adolescent during which parents use many of the same skills learned in the play sessions. The play sessions or special times are dyadic in nature – one parent and one child at a time. This format permits optimal relationship development and attention to the child's needs. Ideally, all children in the family become involved in play sessions or special times with their parents.

WHAT IS FILIAL THERAPY?

Filial Therapy is a form of family therapy. It is based on a psycho-educational model rather than a medical or expert model of practice. It harnesses the power of play therapy within the family context to empower children, parents, and the family as a whole. It helps children, parents, and families make changes that lead to closer, more cohesive relationships and better individual and collective adjustment.

The term "filial therapy" comes from the Latin filios or filias, technically meaning sons or daughters. Loosely translated, it means parent-child. As Filial Therapy evolved, the Guerneys and others tried to find more user-friendly terms for it (Child Relationship Enhancement Family Therapy, Filial Play Therapy, Filial Family Therapy), but the name Filial Therapy remains the most widely recognized. In 2003, Louise Guerney (personal communication) requested that the term be capitalized when referring specifically to the Guerney model of conducting Filial Therapy, and that the lower case "filial therapy" or other terminology be used to refer to significant variations from the original approach (VanFleet, 2011a). That request is incorporated in this edition.

Filial Therapy refers to a theoretically integrative form of therapy in which practitioners train and supervise parents (or other caregivers) as they conduct special nondirective play sessions with their own children. The therapist provides feedback to the parents to aid in the development of their competence and confidence. Using a collaborative approach, therapists also discuss children's play themes with parents, helping parents understand their children's motivations, feelings, intentions, and behaviors in context. As parents develop the skills for conducting and understanding their play sessions, the therapist helps them shift the play sessions to the home environment. At this point the therapist continues to monitor the play sessions and overall progress with weekly or biweekly meetings with the parents alone. The therapist also helps parents generalize what they have learned to daily life and parenting situations (VanFleet, 2011a).

Filial Therapy is considered a time-limited intervention, typically requiring 15 to 20 one-hour sessions for families experiencing moderately challenging problems. It was originally developed as group family therapy, and it is still conducted as such today when feasible (L. F. Guerney & Ryan, 2013). The length of family therapy-oriented groups ranges from 16 to 24 weeks, and there are several parenting-skills-type group adaptations that run from 8 to 12 weeks. These will be outlined later in this volume. Filial Therapy easily can be used with individual families, and this book focuses on that process. Therapists can use Filial Therapy for prevention work as well as an intervention for seriously distressed children and families.

THEORETICAL INTEGRATION

Much of the section that follows first appeared in a three-part article series, Filial Therapy: What Every Play Therapist Should Know, that appeared in the *Play Therapy Magazine of the British Association of Play Therapists* (VanFleet, 2011a,b,c) and is reprinted with slight modification here with their permission.

The heart and soul of any form of therapy depends on the theories and assumptions behind it. To truly understand an intervention, one must understand its foundations. When Bernard Guerney began detailing his idea of having parents conduct nondirective play sessions with their own children under the supervision of a therapist, he pulled what he considered to be the strongest aspects of several theories of human psychology (personal communication). Filial Therapy represents a true synthesis of features of psychodynamic, humanistic, interpersonal, behavioral, developmental, cognitive, and family systems theories. For example, while parents learn to show acceptance and unconditional positive regard to their children, they also provide clear behavioral limits and consequences for unsafe or destructive behaviors. While therapists teach parents using reinforcement and social learning theories, they also convey considerable empathy and support to the parents. The contributions of these theories for children and parents in Filial Therapy are described below and in greater detail in several sources (Cavedo & B.G. Guerney, 1999; Ginsberg, 2003; L. F. Guerney, 1997, 2003b; L.F. Guerney & Ryan, 2013; VanFleet, 2009a).

Psychodynamic. From psychodynamic theory, Filial Therapy pulls a recognition of the importance of the unconscious and of defense mechanisms, and highlights their importance for developing self-understanding and growth. Catharsis offers release and healing, while Adlerian psychology emphasizes the need for goals, mastery, and social interest. It is assumed that children's play during Filial Therapy reveals their inner worlds, including their anxieties and their hopes. Their play is considered symbolic and meaningful. From the parents' perspective, children's play themes reflect matters of family dynamics. Children's play within the safety of the parent-child play sessions helps parents see dynamic issues, not only for the child, but for themselves and the entire family. The therapist helps parents work through these insights so that families can reach goals that yield better adjustment for all family members and the family as a whole.

Humanistic. Filial Therapy applies humanistic, and specifically, Rogerian, theory amply throughout its process. Filial Therapy aims to enhance each family member's self-concept through the use of acceptance, genuine respect, and empathy. Children receive positive regard from their parents during the nondirective, child-centered play sessions. Parents learn to provide genuine acceptance and empathy for the children's feelings, thoughts, and motives. It is a key feature of Filial Therapy that practitioners provide this same type of safe and accepting environment to convey understanding of parents' feelings, thoughts, conflicts, and desires. Deep levels of empathy are essential for the effective engagement of parents in the process, and understanding and acceptance help parents make the sometimes difficult but necessary changes for a more satisfying family life. Filial Therapy represents a chain of empathy, giving to parents the same acceptance the therapist helps them provide for their children and each other.

Behavioral. Filial Therapy employs principles and methods from behaviorism and learning theory, including the use of teaching methods that ensure success. There are behavioral components within the play sessions for children, where the structuring and limit-setting skills add security, boundaries, and clear consequences to eliminate unwanted child behaviors. Parents learn a balanced approach to parenting. Therapists use reinforcement, shaping, and vicarious learning to help parents master new skills and behaviors for use with their children. The parent training process heavily depends on behavior and learning principles (VanFleet, 2009b).

Interpersonal. Filial Therapy is based on the premise that individual behavior is largely influenced by interpersonal experiences. Sullivan's (1947) circumplex model of interpersonal theory suggests that one's reactions are closely associated with and influenced by other people's behaviors and reactions. Filial Therapy seeks to alter the action-reaction pairings that are common in the parent-child relationship by helping parents bring them to awareness and select different ways of acting or reacting to circumstances or each other. Also of great importance in Filial Therapy is the idea, drawn from interpersonal theory, that paying attention to the reciprocal nature of parent-child relationships during play sessions helps both parent and child take responsibility for changes, resulting in more satisfying family relationships overall.

Cognitive. Cognitive therapy is based on the idea that what we think affects how we feel and how we behave. In Filial Therapy, it is believed that nondirective play sessions help children change the way they think about themselves, others, and the world. This occurs as children play, expressing different feelings and acting out different roles, identities, and scenarios through their imaginary play. As often happens in the parent-child play sessions of traumatized children, they might put themselves in an imaginary victim role in the early play sessions, but increasingly assume more powerful roles that eventually vanquish the "bad guys" as their play progresses. Practitioners also help parents think differently about their children and themselves. When parents react to themes that arise in their children's play, therapists help them sort out their thoughts and help them reframe their understanding of the situation. For example, many parents start therapy thinking that their children are deliberately trying to anger them, but they often leave Filial Therapy without this belief, having replaced it with a more realistic and compassionate understanding of how trauma or anxiety drives behavior.

Developmental/Attachment. Children's feelings and behaviors are deeply influenced by their developmental levels and attachment experiences. Children's play during Filial Therapy sessions often reflects developmental tasks relevant to them at the time, such as when a 5-year-old pours water back and forth ad infinitum, demonstrating developmental mastery at work. Therapists help parents understand developmental features when they emerge in the play and help parents set more realistic expectations or become more accepting. Attachment issues also arise naturally in the play, such as when a child from an enmeshed, insecure attachment relationship does not invite her mother to play any roles with her. The therapist often must reassure the parent that this is not worrisome at all, but a good thing. The play opens the discussion between therapist and parent, and the therapist can explain how healthy attachment involves episodes of child exploration and independence followed by a return to the secure base. In this way, even parental attachment dilemmas can be raised, discussed, and modified (BiFulco & Thomas, 2012). Filial Therapy empowers all family members in such a way that they can feel emotionally safe enough to shift to healthier attachment styles and ways of relating. Even severe problems associated with trauma and attachment disruption can be addressed successfully by Filial Therapy because of the way it addressed both trauma and attachment dynamics within the same intervention.

Family Systems. From a theoretical perspective, the client in Filial Therapy is neither the child nor the parent, but the relationship that exists between them and among all family members. When one part of the family changes, it affects the entire family system, so Filial Therapy practitioners try to include all members of the family whenever possible. Although play sessions are held between one parent and one child at a time, the entire family is involved in the process. Therapists stay alert to changes at all levels within the family system, and consider the broader systems within which the family is embedded, such as extended family, school, work, neighborhood, and culture (Bronfenbrenner, 1979). The incorporation of family systems theories in Filial Therapy are covered in greater depth elsewhere (Topham & VanFleet, 2011; VanFleet & Topham, 2011).

PSYCHOEDUCATIONAL MODEL

One might wonder how these different theories reside happily together in one intervention. They hardly share similar assumptions and practices. The answer lies in the essential nature of the model used, which is a psychoeducational one. Psychoeducational models assume that most problems arise for individuals and their families due to a lack of knowledge or skill. The family's repertoire of parenting or relationship skills is not sufficient to meet all family members' needs or to address the stressors the family is facing. Psychoeducational interventions are designed to teach and assist family members in applying the knowledge and skills that will help them resolve their problems. This is fundamentally different from expert models or the medical model on which so many therapeutic services are based.

The Guerneys and their colleagues (Andronico et al., 1967) discussed the didactic and dynamic elements of Filial Therapy early in its development. Louise Guerney (1997) described

> the dual commitment to the forthright teaching of play sessions and simultaneous focus on the parents' feelings as players and on parents as parents. . . . In involving parents in this process, one is entering the potentially emotionally threatening world of the parent-child relationship – a world of feelings and attitudes and family dynamics that would require the same respect and understanding that parents were asked to provide for their children. It should be understood, however, that the task of working with the children is always given top priority and the parents' feelings and personal concerns never dominate. Filial Therapy is not a circuitous route to providing client-centered personal or parental therapy to parents. The perspectives of parents are critical and require acceptance and understanding on the way to learning how to develop the competence to conduct an appropriate child-centered play session for the benefit of their children and their relationships with their children. (pp. 131-132).

Therapists who practice Filial Therapy serve as clinicians and educators, developmental specialists and family therapists. A clear understanding of the theoretically integrative nature of this approach and its competence-oriented psychoeducational framework are essential for best practices in Filial Therapy (VanFleet, 2011a).

CORE VALUES OF FILIAL THERAPY

Related to the theories that comprise it, there are a number of core values of Filial Therapy (Ginsberg, 2003; L. F. Guerney, 1997, 2003b; L. F. Guerney & Ryan, 2013; VanFleet, 2004). Filial therapists embrace these values and incorporate them into their work at all times. They are listed below.

- Honesty – the therapist is honest with clients at all times and creates an environment that encourages clients to be honest with their families

- Openness – the therapist shares information and impressions openly with clients. There are no "hidden agendas" or thoughts in the process, as they could damage the relationship. The therapist shares with clients the values on which the process is based and discusses them in terms of the clients' own value systems.
- Respect – the therapist shows respect for the clients while expecting them to show respect for each other.
- Genuineness – the therapist seeks to be genuine, to truly be him- or herself in all interactions with clients.
- Empathy, understanding, acceptance – the therapist seeks to understand clients at a deep level through the use of acceptance and empathy. In turn, the therapist works with parents to convey empathy and acceptance with their children.
- Relationship – the focus of the intervention is to build stronger relationships. Relationships are viewed as essential to human well-being, and the entire process revolves around building strong therapeutic relationships while helping clients build strong family relationships.
- Empowerment, self-efficacy, education – the therapist seeks to build clients' knowledge and skills in an effort to empower them. Client input is viewed as essential and is always encouraged. The entire process focuses on helping clients make decisions and to be as self-sufficient as possible through the use of skill-building and support.
- Humility – the therapist maintains humility, with a recognition that clients have much information and many strengths that can be harnessed to solve their own problems. The therapist might be considered an expert on the specific skills and methods taught to clients, but clients are viewed as the experts on their own lives.
- Collaboration – the therapist treats parents as true partners in the process. At all stages, the therapist consults with clients about decisions, goals, steps forward, and concerns. Parents' input is sought and valued on par with the therapist's own thoughts and ideas.
- Playfulness and humor – the therapist values a playful, light atmosphere and tries to create this for the parents, just as parents learn to create a playful, safe, and accepting climate for their

children. Humor is used frequently, and only in an affirming way.

- Emotional expression – expression of feelings is considered important for all family members. The therapist encourages emotional expression in an empathic environment, in order to enhance understanding within the family and the therapeutic process.
- Family strength – the therapist strives to help families become stronger through the use of all the values listed here.
- Balance – the process eschews extreme positions and instead focuses on balancing the necessary aspects of child rearing, such as the need to balance freedom and choices with limits and boundaries.

ESSENTIAL FEATURES OF FILIAL THERAPY

The theoretical underpinnings and the values discussed above culminate in the essential features of Filial Therapy (i.e., those elements that make it unique). In recent years, other interventions have been developed that involve parents with their children and that use play as a modality, but they can be quite unlike Filial Therapy, even though these two elements are similar. Because of Filial Therapy's rich tapestry of theoretical influences and the Guerneys' creativity and wisdom in weaving them together, it is rare to find forms of therapy even today that so artfully integrate the relative strengths of so many orientations in such a pragmatic and powerful tool to help children and families.

This section identifies the principles central to the conduct of Filial Therapy. It is the combination of these essential elements that defines Filial Therapy as a distinct form of therapy (VanFleet, 2011b). These features can be found individually or in smaller combinations in other interventions, but it is the presence of all of them that defines Filial Therapy as originally conceptualized by the Guerneys and practiced by them and their students throughout the past half-century (VanFleet, 2011a). Other formats inspired by Filial Therapy sometimes omit one or two of the essential features, but they are still considered part of the family of Filial Therapy because they include most of them and have altered their stated objectives or scope accordingly. More information about these adaptations is provided later in this volume. The essential features follow.

The importance of play in child development is highlighted, and play is seen as the primary avenue for gaining greater understanding of children. Through play, children express their feelings, master new skills, integrate new experiences into their understanding of their world, develop social judgment, and hone their problem-solving and coping abilities. Filial therapists believe that play is therapeutically beneficial for children. The same principles that guide the practice of child-centered, or nondirective, play therapy guide the play sessions that parents learn to hold with their own children (see VanFleet, Sywulak, & Sniscak, 2010 for a thorough review).

Parents are empowered as the change agents for their own children. Filial Therapy is based on the assumption that parents are the most significant adults in children's lives and are likely to have a greater impact on their children than any therapist could. The method is further grounded in the belief that most parents are capable of learning the skills necessary to conduct the child-centered play sessions and help their children. When parents learn more effective ways of interacting with and helping their children, the positive results are likely to be more profound and longer lasting. Filial Therapy is a form of family therapy that seeks to help the family system attain higher levels of functioning through this empowerment. Parents are seen and involved as true partners in the therapeutic process.

The client is the relationship, not the individual. Current systems of care often emphasize the identification of a single client, and that frequently is the child. Parents often come to therapy or are referred because of the behavior of one of their children. To focus on that individual child, however, runs the risk of missing the root of the problem, which often lies embedded within the family dynamic, such as marital tension, poor parenting practices, illness or death within the family, maltreatment, imbalanced or chaotic family organization, poor economic conditions, or attachment difficulties. Rarely do problems arise solely from a single child. Even problems that are centered within the child, such as ADHD with its biological underpinnings, influence the entire family and the psychosocial problems encountered in various ways by all family members. A child with a chronic medical illness such as diabetes might exhibit behavior or medical compliance problems, but the management of that illness rests heavily on the parents, and siblings can lose parental attention if the medical situation demands much of the family's time.

In Filial Therapy, neither the child nor the parents are viewed as the primary client. Practitioners focus on the relationships that develop between parents and their children, as well as among all family members. Filial Therapy is designed to strengthen those relationships and to resolve weaknesses that threaten them. From a practical point of view, therapists sometimes must identify a single client for payment or reporting purposes, so a parent or a child might be listed as the "official" client, but the well-being of the parent-child relationship remains foremost in practitioners' minds and guides all decision-making.

Empathy is essential for growth and change. Empathy is considered to be critical in the formation of healthy social bonds and mutually satisfying relationships (Perry & Szalavitz, 2010). It helps establish the attunement necessary for secure attachments, and it is within the context of safe, accepting relationships that growth is nurtured. In Filial Therapy, empathy plays a prominent role on several levels. Filial practitioners must be highly skilled in providing empathy to adults and children alike. They provide genuineness and acceptance through their empathic listening abilities. Therapists provide empathy at the parent level by truly trying to see things through parents' eyes without judgment. They empathically listen to the deepest levels of parent feelings and concerns and convey acceptance. This does not mean that they accept or approve of parents' prior bad acts, but they accept the parents' underlying emotions, motivations, and hopes. While a therapist would never condone a parent's use of spanking or hurting a child, they would try to understand the parent's frustration or rage that fueled that behavior. Deep understanding of parent feelings typically results in greater parent engagement in the therapeutic process, enhancing the potential for positive parent change. Empathic listening with parents is not a simple restatement of their thoughts and feelings; rather, it is a commitment to understanding parent feelings at the deepest level possible. An example would be if a parent asserted, "Sometimes I just can't stand that kid. I know it sounds awful, but he's hateful!" If the therapist responded, "You're upset with him," it would be considered empathic, but it fails to reflect the intensity of the parent's feelings. A deeper empathic response would be, "You're furious with him and feel at the end of your rope!" In Filial Therapy, practitioners use empathy and acceptance with parents throughout the process.

At the child level, Filial therapists must first become proficient in child-centered play therapy (VanFleet et al., 2010). In the early stages of Filial Therapy, they typically provide demonstrations of child-centered play sessions with each of the family's children while parents observe. Therapists must be able to empathize with and reflect children's feelings at the deepest level. They recognize that surface behaviors, such as aggression or oppositionality, are often driven by more fundamental feelings and motivations beneath the surface, such as fear and anxiety, and they respond empathically to all levels to convey true acceptance. Through their training and experience, Filial therapists know what to expect in child-centered play therapy and how to recognize and interpret play themes within developmental and psychosocial contexts. In essence, they must practice what they preach.

Finally, the parent-child play sessions throughout Filial Therapy remain nondirective in nature. Parents do not switch to more direct behaviors such as positive reinforcement at any point during the play sessions, as this represents a fundamental shift away from the empathy and acceptance considered critical for relationship-building and parent-child change. While therapists help parents use skills such as positive reinforcement and parent messages in daily life, these are never brought into the play sessions, which remain child-centered.

The use of empathic listening in Filial Therapy belies an essential belief that people – children and adults – will move in the direction of psychosocial health when an atmosphere of safety, understanding, and acceptance is created for them. In many ways, empathy is the cornerstone of the Filial Therapy model because it defines so much of the therapist-family and the parent-child relationships.

The entire family is involved whenever possible. Filial Therapy was conceived as family therapy, although family psychology was just emerging at the same time. This means that all of the relationships within the family are of importance to practitioners. Therapists encourage both parents to participate in the process, including observations of each other's play sessions and feedback. They learn vicariously from this. It is common to hear one parent use some of the same phrases and reflections they heard the other parent use in a previous play session. Efforts are made to bring reluctant parents into Filial Therapy, assuring them of the importance of their input and their value to their children. Because both parents or caregivers learn the same balanced approach of empathy and boundaries, Filial Therapy often brings parents with radically different parenting styles to a central place. The disciplinarian learns also how to be understanding. The nurturing parent becomes firmer with limits. It is precisely because of this process that parents, from the earliest days of Filial Therapy, have reported that their marriages seem to improve because they are more in tune with each other vis-à-vis parenting matters.

Practitioners using Filial Therapy also try to include all of the children in the process. For adolescents, this means the inclusion of "special times" instead of play sessions as a means of providing undivided parental attention, understanding, structure, and enjoyment on a regular basis. For children between the ages of 2 and 12 (approximately), Filial Therapy works best when they are all included in weekly or biweekly one-to-one play sessions with their parents. As noted earlier, the problems that bring families to therapy affect all family members. Behavioral challenges with one child can easily draw parental attention away from siblings who do not show problems. Divorce may result in one child acting out while the quieter child is viewed as "doing just fine," when in actuality that child is depressed, withdrawn, or anxious. True to its family systems roots, Filial therapists advocate that all children be included somehow. Ideally, this would be from the start of therapy, but because of practical limitations in current models of service delivery, it might require therapist creativity in how to include all the children in the process.

It is quite common in Filial Therapy for parents to be more challenged during the play sessions by the child they originally thought had no problems. Involving all children in play sessions pays dividends that strengthen the family as a whole. Parents seem to learn the skills more quickly and solidly when they hold play sessions with each of their children. Perhaps holding play sessions with different child personalities and issues strengthens parents' use of the skills, just as experience with more than one child enhances a clinician's competence and effectiveness. At other times, parents who feel challenged by one child during play sessions can be encouraged when their play sessions with other children go well.

A psychoeducational training model is used with parents. Biologically based problems are certainly recognized and treated as such, but Filial therapists tend to view most social, emotional, and behavioral difficulties of children and their families as environmentally based adjustment problems arising primarily from a lack of knowledge or skill. Education and skill development can therefore alleviate many problems, yielding therapeutic benefits.

Filial Therapy uses a training model for parents that has been shown to lead to successful acquisition of the necessary skills. The model is comprised of four elements: (a) explanation and rationale of the skill, (b) demonstration of the skill, (c) skills practice, and (d) individualized feedback. Therapists explain the rationale and methods of each skill taught to parents, answering any questions as they arise. They then demonstrate those skills in action through at least one child-centered play therapy session with each of the family's children while the parents observe. Discussions after the observed sessions help parents process their observations, questions, and doubts about the process and its relevance to their family.

Therapists then train parents through the use of skills practice, including tried-and-true behavioral and learning methods. Initially this takes the form of mock play sessions in which the therapist role-plays a child while the parent uses the play session skills. The therapist matches the level of difficulty of the child they role-play to each parent's current ability, gradually increasing the challenge until the parent is fully trained. Therapists' use of in-the-moment encouragement applies the behavioral shaping principle to give parents immediate feedback on their efforts, reduce their performance anxiety, and assist in the learning process. This teaching process helps most parents acquire the skills rather quickly.

After each mock session, the therapist provides more detailed feedback, the majority of which focuses on things the parent did well, adding just one or two things for the parent to try to improve the next time. The individualized feedback helps parents learn rapidly by combining a supportive and collaborative climate with specific information about their use of the skills. Parents are given ample opportunity to discuss their own feelings in order to clear out misconceptions, to eliminate obstacles to progress, and to give them "ownership" of their own learning. This same process is applied after parents start their play sessions with their own children.

Tangible support and continued learning are provided through live supervision of parents' early play sessions with their children. A key feature of Filial Therapy is to create the circumstances through which parents are successful. One of the problems of traditional parenting skills programs is that parents are exposed briefly to a new skill, such as listening, and are then asked to use it immediately at home. It is not uncommon for parents to return to the next session saying, "I tried it and it didn't work." While it is tempting to think this response is due to lack of parent motivation, it is more likely the result of a parent trying to implement a skill they have not yet mastered in a very complex environment – daily life. Filial Therapy bypasses this difficulty by asking parents to refrain from using the skills in everyday life until they have mastered them during the play sessions. Filial therapists then observe parents' first four to six play sessions directly, often by sitting unobtrusively in the corner of the playroom. This gives the therapist a three-dimensional vantage point to see the full sessions, parents' skill usage, child responses, and interpersonal nuances that occur. It also offers parents tacit support as they begin to apply their new learning with their children.

After the half-hour play session, the children are excused to a safe childcare location, and the therapist goes through the feedback process with the parents. Parents are first invited to reflect on their own use of the skills; "What was easy for you?" "What was difficult?" The therapist empathizes with their responses and then offers skills feedback in the form of positive reinforcement for specific behaviors and one or two suggestions for improvement: "Jennie, when you kept describing what your daughter was feeding all her baby dolls – the juice and the coffee – you were doing such a nice job reflecting the content of her play! Next time, see if you can bring out her feelings a bit more, such as, "You think it's funny that babies would drink coffee."

After four to six sessions of live supervision, parents have typically developed their competence and confidence to an extent they can begin their home sessions. The therapist provides indirect supervision of these, based on parent reports and/or home videos. It is this supervisory support that helps parents succeed, build their skills, and maintain their motivation as they shift some of their characteristic ways of responding to their children.

The process is truly collaborative. In every way possible, practitioners of Filial Therapy involve parents as partners in the therapeutic process. It is a misconception, however, that Filial Therapy teaches parents to become therapists. The Filial therapist retains responsibility for the therapy for the duration of family involvement, while parents are learning a set of play session skills that, when eventually generalized from the play sessions to daily life, have been shown to improve parenting practices and parent-child relationships significantly. It is the therapist's responsibility to monitor and manage the therapeutic process in its many complexities.

With that said, Filial therapists welcome and encourage parent input at every step of the way. What parents think, feel, and say matters. Whether they are reflecting on their own play sessions or trying to determine the possible meanings of their children's play, parents' views are elicited and discussed first, with the therapist adding his or her own ideas afterwards. Therapists consider and use parents' perceptions, realizing that parents know the child's context much better than they, and that parent ideas about the meaning of the play is significant because of this. Therapists freely acknowledge that parents' insights can be more relevant than their own.

The relationship between a practitioner and a parent during Filial Therapy is decidedly collegial: sharing of ideas, listening, collaboratively deciding on options, mutual respect, and laughter. Metaphorically, it is the difference between sitting side by side or in an open circle for Filial groups discussing an issue of mutual concern (partnership) and sitting across a desk or table doing the same (expert model). The climate of Filial Therapy is one of open, friendly teamwork.

GOALS OF FILIAL THERAPY

Filial Therapy has potential benefits for both children and parents. Therapeutic goals for children include the following:

1. To enable children to recognize and express their feelings fully and constructively.
2. To give children the opportunity to be heard.
3. To help children develop effective problem-solving and coping skills.
4. To increase children's self-confidence and self-esteem.
5. To increase children's trust and confidence in their parents.
6. To reduce or eliminate maladaptive behaviors and presenting problems.
7. To help children develop proactive and prosocial behaviors.
8. To promote secure attachment relationships and an open, cohesive family climate that fosters healthy and balanced child development in all spheres: social, emotional, intellectual, behavioral, physical, and spiritual.

Therapeutic goals for parents in Filial Therapy include the following:

1. To increase parents' understanding of child development in general.
2. To increase parents' understanding of their own children in particular.
3. To help parents recognize the importance of play and emotion in their children's lives as well as in their own.
4. To decrease parents' feelings of frustration with their children.
5. To aid parents in the development of a variety of skills that are likely to yield better child-rearing outcomes.
6. To increase parents' confidence in their ability to parent.
7. To help parents open the doors of communication with their children and then keep them open.
8. To enable parents to work together better as a team.
9. To increase parents' feelings of warmth and trust toward their children.
10. To provide a nonthreatening atmosphere in which parents may deal with their own issues as they relate to their children and parenting.

Overall, Filial Therapy aims to (a) eliminate the presenting problems at their source, (b) develop positive interactions, attachments, and relationships between parents and their children, and (c) increase families' communication, coping, and problem-solving skills so they are better able to handle future problems independently and successfully.

The sections that follow in this guide start with an overview of the research followed by an explanation of the rationale for using child-centered play sessions in Filial Therapy. Methods and issues in the assessment of families for Filial Therapy are followed by specific approaches to training parents to conduct play sessions. The course of therapy is followed chronologically: (a) assessment, (b) training, (c) initial play sessions, (d) therapist-supervised play sessions, (e) transfer of play sessions to the home setting, (f) generalization of skills, and (g) closing. A case study is used to illustrate the various phases of Filial Therapy.* Finally, alternative formats and applications of Filial Therapy to specialized populations are briefly described.

---

*In order to protect client privacy, this case study is a composite of several different families. The clinical problems, family dynamics, and interventions realistically illustrate Filial Therapy principles, however.

FILIAL THERAPY RESEARCH

Research on Filial Therapy began with its inception and continues to the present. L. F. Guerney (2000, 2003a, 2003b; L. F. Guerney & Ryan, 2013) provides an historical perspective on the development of Filial Therapy and the research that helped shape it. VanFleet, Ryan, and Smith (2005) have reviewed the empirical history and ongoing research. Because Filial Therapy is an empirically derived, evidence-based approach, an overview of its research is included here.

When B. G. Guerney (1964) first described Filial Therapy in the *Journal of Consulting Psychology* and other journals, the professional psychological community reacted with skepticism. Questions were raised about its effectiveness and appropriateness. Some had difficulty believing that parents could actually learn the play session skills and worried about the misuse of psychological methods. These objections were tested in a series of early studies on Filial Therapy. Andronico and B. G. Guerney (1969) and Stover and B. G. Guerney (1967) studied whether parents could competently conduct nondirective play sessions with their own children. Parents and therapists were trained to conduct the play sessions. Trained observers, who were not informed whether they were viewing a parent or a therapist, then rated play sessions on specific behavioral measures. No significant differences were found in therapist and parent skill levels. This research indicated that parents could become competent in the conduct of play sessions.

These early studies were followed by a nationally funded research project that thoroughly examined a wide range of process and outcome variables (B. G. Guerney & Stover, 1971). The researchers explored the types of families and problems that could be addressed with Filial Therapy, as well as therapy formats; the psychometric properties of instruments used to evaluate Filial Therapy; emotional, behavioral, and adjustment changes in the children; and parental satisfaction, empathy, and skill changes. The study included 51 mothers of children 3 to 10 years old with serious emotional difficulties. The families participated in a small group format for 12 to 18 months. Multiple indices included ratings of over 60,000 play session behaviors. Results indicated that the mothers increased their satisfaction with their children and improved their empathy for their children. The children's problem behaviors decreased while social adjustment increased. This was a thorough exploratory study, but it did not include a control group as that would have been premature at this point of development of the approach.

Oxman (1972) provided a comparison study, using the 51 mothers of the B. G. Guerney and Stover (1971) study as her experimental group. She then established a general population, matched, no-treatment control group of 77 mothers to compare the data. Mothers who participated in Filial Therapy reported significantly more improvement in their children's behavior and significantly greater satisfaction with their children than mothers in the comparison group. A follow-up study of 42 of the original 51 mothers (L. F. Guerney, 1975) showed that 86% of the gains from Filial Therapy were maintained 1 to 3 years after discharge from therapy. Over three-quarters of the mothers continued to report significantly more satisfaction with their children.

These early foundational studies were followed by increasingly more controlled studies of Filial Therapy. Sywulak (1977) studied 32 parents who served as their own controls. Data were collected during a 4-month waiting period preceding treatment, at the start of treatment, after 2 months of treatment, and after 4 months of Filial Therapy. Parents of children with a wide range of presenting problems became significantly more accepting of their children during the first 2 months of Filial Therapy, with the greatest improvements made during this time. Improvements continued through 4 months of treatment. Similarly, gains in children's overall adjustment and specific presenting problems were significant after 2 and 4 months of Filial Therapy. Study results showed improvements in children's aggression problems, withdrawn behaviors, and others. As with their earlier studies, parents in this study reported high levels of satisfaction with filial therapy, indicating that it contributed to their feelings of competence as parents and to many benefits in their relationships with their children. Sensue (1981) conducted a 3-year follow-up study of the parents in the Sywulak study. She developed a comparison sample from the friends of the parents who had participated in Filial Therapy. Results indicated that parents who had participated in Filial Therapy showed significant improvements in parental acceptance and child adjustment lasting 3 years, as compared with their pretreatment data as well as with comparison group parents.

As the popularity of Filial Therapy has grown, so has the amount of research being conducted on it. Studies have explored its efficacy using a variety of formats with a range of presenting problems. Filial Therapy has been studied with different cultural groups throughout the United States and the world. Numerous studies with waiting list control groups have been conducted as doctoral dissertations and through grant projects (VanFleet et al., 2005). Filial Therapy has consistently been shown to improve parental acceptance, child adjustment, parental stress, and family satisfaction, even in quite short-term adaptations. For example, its effectiveness has been demonstrated with single and divorced parents (Bratton & Landreth, 1995), child conduct behavior problems (Johnson-Clark, 1996), chronically ill children (Glazer-Waldman, 1991; Tew, 1997), nonoffending parents of sexually abused children (Costas & Landreth, 1999), children with learning disabilities (Kale & Landreth, 1999), families of domestic violence (Barabash, 2003; Smith, 2000), and incarcerated mothers (Harris & Landreth, 1995) and fathers (Landreth & Lobaugh, 1998). Its adaptability and effectiveness have also been demonstrated with different cultural groups within the United States and abroad: Native Americans (Glover & Landreth, 2000), Korean families in Korea (Jang, 2000) and Korean immigrants in the United States (Lee, 2003), Chinese families (Chau & Landreth, 1997), and German mothers and children (Grskovic & Goetze, 2008). Detailed case studies have highlighted the value of and need for Filial Therapy for children with attachment-related problems (Ryan, 2004; VanFleet & Sniscak, 2003a) and other family systems issues, such as blended families (Hutton, 2004).

A meta-analysis of play therapy and Filial Therapy research (Bratton et al., 2005) indicated that parents in Filial Therapy performed 1.06 to 1.15 standard deviations better than nontreatment groups. This study clearly indicated that parent involvement, especially in the Filial Therapy process, had strong advantages over play therapy interventions conducted individually with children, which were also shown to be effective.

Research on Filial Therapy continues to widen, with studies being conducted at universities throughout the United States, Canada, the United Kingdom, China, Korea, South Africa, and other countries. Program evaluation studies are also being conducted within community mental health centers, adoption programs, foster care and family re-unification programs, Head Start agencies, independent practice settings, and with many different cultural groups.

A recent study (Topham et al., 2011) of 27 parent-child dyads examined the predictors of treatment success in Filial Therapy. They found that higher levels of parent distress and poorer child regulation of emotion at pre-test were predictive of significant reductions in child behavior problems across treatment. Poor emotion regulation in parents at pre-test was predictive of significant increases in parental acceptance across treatment. Although studies have not yet examined whether Filial

Therapy leads to improvement in parent and child emotion regulation, this study indicates that parents and children with poorer emotion regulation are likely to experience positive gains in Filial Therapy. From this, one can speculate that the positive changes are a function of improving emotion regulation. The study also found that lower parent satisfaction with social support from family and friends at pre-test was predictive of greater improvements in parental communication of acceptance during parent-child play. It is possible that this finding is the result of the richly supportive environment that Filial Therapy offers to parents. This study is the first known to explore the role of metaemotion variables as predictors of outcome in Filial Therapy, and to look beyond the question of "Is Filial Therapy effective?" to "For whom is Filial Therapy effective?" This informative and promising line of research is continuing.

The development of Filial Therapy for child and family treatment has been intertwined with research from its earliest days. Empirical studies helped shape the Filial Therapy method itself, and a body of research has grown that consistently demonstrates its effectiveness and applicability. Studies have shown its long-term benefits for children and families, making it a robust intervention for a wide range of problems, as well as an effective preventive modality.

The sections that follow provide details about the Filial Therapy process.

CHILD-CENTERED PLAY SESSIONS

Filial Therapy teaches parents to conduct child-centered play sessions with their own children. This section describes the nature of child-centered play therapy. More detailed information is available in VanFleet et al. (2010).

PRINCIPLES OF CHILD-CENTERED PLAY THERAPY

In a child-centered play session, the child is in charge of the play. The child selects the toys to play with and the manner of play. The child-centered play therapist continually shows acceptance of the child's actions and feelings through the ongoing use of empathic listening. The therapist imposes few rules or limits in order to create an open atmosphere in which the child feels comfortable expressing his or her true feelings. When necessary, the therapist sets and enforces limits in a defined, effective manner so the child understands the boundaries and learns to take responsibility for his or her actions. The therapist engages in play with the child only when the child requests it, and then does so in the manner desired by the child. At all times, the therapist follows the eight basic principles of nondirective, child-centered play therapy according to Axline (1947, 1969):

1. The therapist must develop a warm, friendly relationship with the child, in which good rapport is established as soon as possible.
2. The therapist accepts the child exactly as he is.
3. The therapist establishes a feeling of permissiveness in the relationship so that the child feels free to express his feelings completely.
4. The therapist is alert to recognize the feelings the child is expressing and reflects those feelings back to him in such a manner that he gains insight into his behavior.
5. The therapist maintains a deep respect for the child's ability to solve his own problems if given an opportunity to do so. The responsibility to make choices and institute change is the child's.
6. The therapist does not attempt to direct the child's actions or conversation in any manner. The child leads the way; the therapist follows.
7. The therapist does not attempt to hurry the therapy along. It is a gradual process and is recognized as such by the therapist.
8. The therapist establishes only those limitations that are necessary to anchor the therapy to the world of reality and to make the child aware of his responsibility in the relationship. (Axline, 1969, pp. 73-74)

Filial Therapy employs a child-centered model of play therapy for several reasons: First, child-centered play therapy is straightforward and relatively simple for parents to learn. Second, it provides parents with training and experience in showing empathy to their children on the one hand and the effective use of limits and consequences on the other. Both of these important skills are combined in a comprehensive approach that can be adapted easily to the family's life outside the play sessions. Third, the nondirective nature of the play sessions improves parental attunement and is more likely to build secure attachment relationships between parent and child (Bifulco & Thomas, 2012; Ryan, 2007). A common theme in Filial play sessions is for children to choose exploratory play interspersed with voluntary returns to the "secure base" afforded by the parent. Fourth, Filial therapists model the use of empathic listening skills in their interactions with the parents, and the understanding and acceptance that they convey to the parents helps reduce potential defensiveness. The empathy that parents show to the child when using a child-centered play orientation helps the child develop at his or her own pace and reduces any attempts by the parents to direct or "hurry along" the child's development. Fifth, research (Stover & B. G. Guerney, 1967) and clinical experience have demonstrated that parents can learn to conduct child-centered play sessions with a degree of proficiency comparable to that of professional play therapists.

SELECTION OF TOYS

The selection of toys for a child-centered play therapy room or for a Filial Therapy playroom follows the same principles of Axline (1947, 1969). The Filial therapist furnishes the playroom with toys that encourage the expression of a wide range of feelings and avoids toys that are likely to direct the child's play, such as board games with predetermined rules. (For a thorough explanation of toy selection for child-centered play therapy and Filial Therapy, see VanFleet et al., 2010).

The playroom needs toys that communicate to the child that it is acceptable to express angry or aggressive feelings. The presence of non-look-alike dart guns, a bop bag, a soft rubber knife, and a piece of rope readily indicates to the child that the expression of anger and aggressive play are permitted.

The therapist also makes available toys that are associated with nurturant themes, such as water and bowls, baby bottles, and dolls. Children frequently play out family issues, so the presence of a dollhouse and furniture, a doll family (including mother, father, brother, sister, and baby), a kitchen set with dishes and utensils, and puppets is important.

Construction toys and games that can be used in many ways or that are relatively nondirective are part of a Filial playroom to allow the child's expression of mastery, competition, and cooperation themes. Blocks, ring toss, bean bag toss, cards, and play money are good choices.

Items relating to other common concerns of children, such as medical kits, masks, and a variety of dress-up clothes, are also acceptable. The Filial therapist provides other expressive media such as clay, sand, paper, crayons or markers, and paints.

When considering the inclusion of a particular item in the play-room, the Filial therapist considers three primary factors: (a) whether the item is safe for children, (b) whether it encourages the expression of childhood feelings or themes, and (c) whether the item allows for imaginative or projective use by the child. Toys that are heavily laden with instructions or expectations for their "proper" use are usually re-served for use outside the play sessions. Durability may be an economic consideration as well.

Playroom toys need not be elaborate in order to produce therapeu-tic benefit. This is especially true for Filial Therapy in which parents eventually obtain a special set of toys for play sessions in their own homes. It is probably more important that the therapist presents a mod-est, functional playroom that will not compete with parents' abilities to provide a playroom or area. The therapist scatters the toys throughout the playroom to produce an inviting scene for the children. Items for a typical "starter playroom" are listed below (VanFleet, 2012a, based on L. F. Guerney, 1976b; VanFleet et al., 2010):

Family-Related and Nurturance Toys

doll family (mother, father, brother, sister, baby)
house or box with doll furniture
puppet family/animal puppets
baby doll
baby bottle
dress-up clothes, fabric pieces, hats
container with water
bowls for water play
kitchen dishes

Aggression-Related Toys

inflated bop bag
dart guns with darts (non-look-alike)
small plastic soldiers and/or dinosaurs
6- to 10-foot piece of rope
foam aggression bats or swimming "noodles"
bendable rubber knife
dragon, wolf, and/or other aggressive-looking puppets or toys

Expressive and Construction Toys

crayons or markers with drawing paper
blackboard or whiteboard
blocks or construction toys
Play-Doh, Sculpey, clay, or other modeling substance
small sand tray/container with miniature toys
toy telephones, mobile phones
scarves or bandannas
mirror
masking tape
magic wand
masks
heavy cardboard bricks

Other Multi-Use Toys

deck of cards
play money
medical kit
ring toss or bean bag toss game
cars, trucks, police cars, school bus, ambulance, firetrucks,
    other rescue vehicles

This list can be adapted to include more toys for older children as necessary. Generally, board games are not included and are reserved for child or family play outside the play sessions. Each addition to the playroom should be evaluated in terms of the three factors described earlier. Families do not need all of these items for their home play session kits, but a few items from each category are useful. Filial therapists can help indigent families substitute toy items (VanFleet, 2012a), provide loaner toy kits, and/or offer special toy-making sessions as part of Filial Therapy (Wright & Walker, 2003).

CHILD AND FAMILY
ASSESSMENT FOR FILIAL THERAPY

It is important that therapists carefully assess children and families prior to recommending Filial Therapy. The choice of Filial Therapy, as with all clinical interventions, must be made based upon its ability to meet the family's needs effectively and efficiently.

APPROPRIATE USES OF FILIAL THERAPY

Filial Therapy is appropriate for a wide range of social, emotional, and behavioral problems in children. Problems such as anxiety, depression, reactions to traumatic events, timidity, difficulty getting along with siblings or peers, aggressive acting-out, attention deficit problems, oppositional behaviors, school refusal, enuresis/encopresis, obsessive-compulsive behaviors, reactions to abuse, and attachment difficulties have responded well to Filial Therapy. Specific applications to various populations are discussed on pages 81 to 87.

Filial Therapy is also useful as a preventive approach. It promotes healthy child psychosocial development, strengthens parent-child relationships, provides parents with effective parenting skills, and increases parents' ability to work together better. Many families have enjoyed conducting Filial Therapy play sessions as a means of improving their relationships, preventing potential problems, and having an enjoyable experience together.

Because Filial Therapy has such wide applicability, it is easier, perhaps, to identify situations in which it is not the treatment of choice. There are three general circumstances under which Filial Therapy would be inappropriate as the initial treatment modality. First, it would be inadvisable to use Filial Therapy with parents who are incapable of intellectually comprehending the skills. Modifications of Filial Therapy might be useful in helping such parents learn to understand or play with their children better, but therapeutic expectations of such interventions would need to be realigned with the parents' abilities.

Second, parents who are so overwhelmed by their own needs that they cannot focus on their children's needs probably require therapy for themselves prior to pursuing Filial Therapy. For example, parents who have been devastated by a recent divorce may first need to work through their anger and hurt in individual therapy in order to regain enough emotional energy to help their children. In such cases, the children may require play therapy or some other intervention directly with a professional. Filial Therapy can be more beneficial when it is postponed to a time when the family has the emotional resources needed.

Third, Filial Therapy would not be a viable treatment for abused children when one of the parents has been the perpetrator. The child is unlikely to express his or her innermost feelings in the presence of the perpetrator or the other parent who failed to prevent the abuse from occurring. The child would require individual therapy to work through the trauma and feelings about the parents, and the parents would also need to come to terms with their own behavior. Filial Therapy has been used successfully with such families after the primary abuse issues have been resolved for the child and the parents are ready to learn healthier ways of interacting with their children. Filial Therapy would rarely be considered appropriate for parents who have sexually abused their own children.

THE ASSESSMENT PROCESS

Thorough assessment helps therapists identify the problem accurately and guides them in determining an appropriate match between the client's needs and the recommended therapy. Play diagnostic and assessment approaches are described in Gitlin-Weiner, Sandgrund, and Schaefer (2000), so they will be covered only briefly here. For Filial Therapy, a three-step assessment process works well, although variations are certainly acceptable.

The first step involves a meeting with the parents alone. The therapist empathically listens to the parents' reasons for coming, explores the presenting problem, and obtains full developmental and social histories of the child and family. The therapist also administers any questionnaires, behavior rating scales, or pretests as needed. It is important to obtain as comprehensive a picture as possible of the child's physical, social, emotional, and cognitive development and functioning. The process of engaging parents from the first meeting is illustrated in the DVD by VanFleet (2007).

At the close of the first meeting, the therapist summarizes the parents' concerns, shares any initial reactions with the parents, suggests stop-gap interventions as required, and recommends the second step of assessment, a family play observation. The therapist explains that the family play observation consists of the entire family playing together for approximately 20 to 30 minutes while the therapist watches through a one-way mirror, a closed-circuit television set-up, or as inconspicuously as possible from the corner of the room. Its purpose is to give the therapist a chance to observe the target child interacting with family members and to discuss with the parents afterward how closely the child's observed behavior and interactions resemble those at home.

Finally, the therapist suggests that parents explain to all of their children that the family will be going to a special playroom where they will play together for a while, thereby avoiding any suggestion to the children that they are being taken to see a professional because they've "been bad" or have psychological problems.

The second meeting consists of the actual family play observation. After meeting and chatting with the children, the therapist shows the family into the playroom and then observes through a one-way mirror or as unobtrusively as possible from a location just outside or inside the room. The therapist observes the family, watching for patterns, strengths, and possible problems in the following (L. F. Guerney, no date):

1. Interactions between the target child and each parent.
2. Interactions between the target child and each sibling.
3. Interactions among all children and the parents, the degree of interaction, and the absence of interaction.
4. Locus of control in the family and among the children.
5. Methods used by the target child to achieve his/her goals.
6. Methods used by the parents to control the children.
7. Verbal and nonverbal affective expressions of the target child and possible sources of the feelings.
8. General behavior of the target child, what he/she did.
9. Neurological and other unusual signs, such as distractibility, speech difficulties, or coordination problems in the target child or siblings.
10. Problem interactions between the target child and the others. (p. 69)

During the third step, the therapist meets with the parents alone once again. The parents compare the family play observation with the child's behavior at home, and the therapist shares his or her observations and asks questions. Then the therapist offers short-term guidance for any pressing problems and makes detailed recommendations for therapy, relating them explicitly to the parents' stated concerns.

THE RECOMMENDATION FOR FILIAL THERAPY

When recommending Filial Therapy to parents, the therapist discusses its potential advantages as they relate to the problems the parents have identified. It is important to ensure that the parents understand the importance of play for healthy child development. In a culture where we emphasize the need to "grow up and get serious," the concept that play is a nontrivial, valuable aspect of life might be foreign to some. The therapist discusses the process of Filial Therapy, highlighting the sequence of training for the parents, supervised play sessions, transfer of the play sessions to the home, application of additional parenting skills and interventions, and phased-out termination. Parents must be well informed about the commitment of time and effort Filial Therapy requires: weekly or biweekly therapy sessions for 3 to 6 months with weekly play sessions continuing at home even after therapy has been completed.

The filial therapist responds to parents' questions about the recommendation in a sensitive manner. Empathic listening skills are used liberally to demonstrate understanding of the parents' concerns prior to providing further explanation or rationale. The therapist encourages the parents to express any skepticism they might be feeling in order to deal with it as openly as possible. This, too, is demonstrated in VanFleet's (2007) DVD.

It is at this time that specific goals for therapy are identified and prioritized. The therapist needs to consider and involve the parents as partners in this process. Specific behavioral goals for the child and the parent-child relationship help give the therapy direction and a means of evaluating progress. For "homework," some parents benefit from reading about the rationale, goals, and process of Filial Therapy in *A Parent's Handbook of Filial Therapy* (VanFleet, 2012a) or other descriptive materials.

CASE STUDY: THE TAYLORS

Carol and Ed Taylor were referred for therapy for their 7-year-old daughter, Jessi, by her second-grade teacher. The teacher had reported several behavior problems with Jessi: demanding a great deal of the teacher's time, talking back to the teacher, teasing and bossing her classmates, and alienating herself from her peers.

Carol, a middle-school teacher, and Ed, an accountant, had been married for 10 years. In addition to Jessi, they had a 4-year-old son, Josh. Carol and Ed said that their marriage was generally happy, but they argued about the children and discipline. Ed believed that Carol was too strict with the discipline and that she "nagged" and "bossed" the children too much. Carol felt that Ed was too lenient and uninvolved, leaving the burden of discipline on her.

Both parents agreed that Jessi's behavior had been worsening for the past several years. She had become increasingly "defiant" with them, and she teased Josh "constantly." She had damaged a number of Josh's toys in the past 6 months. They described Jessi as "an instigator, always in trouble." Carol had had training in behavior modification and had tried behavioral programs with Jessi, but Jessi's behavior only seemed to worsen when they gave her more attention. Carol reported several instances when she had praised Jessi for playing quietly with Josh, whereupon Jessi had immediately struck Josh and grabbed the toy he was playing with.

Ed and Carol described Josh as a happy boy who sought out Jessi to play with even though she teased him unmercifully. When she took his toys or poked and pinched him, he cried easily but rarely fought back. They were concerned that he was beginning to allow his playmates to push him around in similar ways. Both children were in good physical health.

The parents described few problems with Jessi prior to Josh's birth. Josh had been a fussy baby requiring much of their attention. They admitted that they had probably neglected Jessi when Josh was a baby. Initially they had tried to involve Jessi in Josh's care, but she had treated him so badly that they eventually kept her separated from him. They were worried that their neglect had resulted in Jessi's current behavior problems. They described Jessi as being quite unhappy with low self-esteem. She frequently told them that she hated herself.

During the family play observation, I (the therapist) noted that Jessi tried several times to shoot Josh with the dart gun. Carol reprimanded her each time, but did not immediately follow through with her threatened consequences. She eventually placed the gun out of reach. Carol corrected Jessi on several other occasions and played a protective role for Josh. Most of the time, when Josh became interested in a new toy, Jessi attempted to play with it herself. Josh gave up the toys with little resistance, and Carol usually intervened to give them back to him. Ed sat in the corner of the room, watching the others with interest but somewhat removed from the play. He tried to call Josh over to play with the toys near him a few times; Josh usually stayed with him briefly and then began exploring the room again.

Ed and Carol believed the family play observation had been quite similar to the family's behavior at home. We further discussed what Ed called the "power struggle" between Jessi and Carol. Carol and Ed expressed an interest in eliminating Jessi's behavior problems and in rebuilding their relationship with her. I recommended Filial Therapy because of the long-standing nature of the problem, Jessi's apparent difficulty in handling a number of emotions (insecurity, jealousy, aggression, and low self-esteem), Ed and Carol's desire to be more consistent with discipline, and their wish to strengthen their relationship with Jessi overall. They agreed to try it.

PARENT TRAINING
PHASE OF FILIAL THERAPY

After the assessment phase, parents are ready to learn the skills necessary to conduct the special play sessions. The Filial therapist introduces four primary skills used in the play sessions, demonstrates them, and then coaches the parents as they practice them in progressively more difficult exercises. It is important that the therapist continually try to model the skills with his or her own behavior during sessions.

The four basic skills are described below, in much the same way the therapist would explain them to parents. (Readers who are less familiar with child-centered play therapy will find the book, *Child-Centered Play Therapy* [VanFleet et al., 2010] useful, as well as the DVD by the same name [VanFleet, 2006a]. The play session skills as detailed in that book and DVD are exactly the same as those taught to parents in Filial Therapy.) The process by which the therapist trains the parents is covered, along with problems that sometimes arise during this phase of therapy.

THE BASIC SKILLS OF FILIAL THERAPY

Structuring Skill. The structuring skill is important to help children understand the overall framework of the play sessions and to help them avoid potential problems. Structuring informs children of general boundaries while maintaining an inviting atmosphere. Children learn through structuring that they will be relatively free to do as they please during the play sessions, but that their parents have authority if the boundaries are not respected. Structuring also helps children distinguish between the special open environment of the play sessions and everyday life with its greater number of restrictions. Finally, by informing children when the play session is nearing the end, the structuring skill gives children the opportunity to finish their play in a manner that is meaningful for them. (It is not unusual for children's play to change rather dramatically in the final minutes of a session when they know time is almost up.)

The Filial therapist explains this rationale for the structuring skill and teaches parents what to say to the child when entering the playroom, how to handle bathroom breaks, and how to end a play session and depart from the playroom.

Entering the Playroom. Parents learn a simple message to say to the child prior to entering the playroom: "(Child's name), this is a very special room. You can do almost anything you want to do in this playroom. If there's something you may not do, I'll let you know."

Bathroom Breaks. The therapist explains to parents that this potential disruption can usually be avoided by allowing the child to use the bathroom prior to entering the playroom. If, however, the child requests a trip to the bathroom, the parent informs the child that he or she may leave the room once in order to go to the bathroom. When the child returns to the playroom, the parent states, "You're back in the special playroom now." This is done to keep the play session boundaries clear.

Playroom Departure. The parents learn to give the child two time warnings as the end of the session nears. Five minutes prior to the end of the session, the parent says, "(Child's name), we have 5 more minutes left in the playroom today." Again at 1 minute prior to the end of the session, the parent tells the child, "(Child's name), we have 1 more minute to play here today." At the end of the session, the parent uses a pleasant but firm tone of voice to say, "(Child's name), our time is up for today. We have to leave the playroom now."

The Filial therapist also teaches parents how to deal with a child who resists or delays leaving the playroom. The parents learn first to reflect the child's feelings and then to restate firmly that the session is over. The parent can also signal that the play session is over by standing up. If needed, the parent takes the child gently by the hand or shoulder and leads him or her out the door. The parent changes his or her demeanor from one of acceptance to one of firmness and finality. The parent goes immediately to the door with the child and ushers him or her out.

Empathic Listening. The Filial therapist also teaches the empathic listening skill to the parents. The therapist explains that this skill will help them show sensitivity and understanding to their children in a way that conveys acceptance of the children's feelings and needs. The empathic listening skill also (a) demonstrates the parents' interest in the children, (b) allows children to clarify any misunderstanding the parents have of their intentions or feelings, (c) provides children with labels for their feelings, thereby increasing their ability to express their emotions in constructive ways, and (d) helps children accept themselves when they feel accepted by their parents.

Parents learn to give the child their undivided attention during the play sessions and to use their own words to rephrase aloud both the content of the play (what the child is doing), and especially the main feelings the child expresses. The therapist illustrates the listening skill with examples and brief demonstrations. The therapist might say, "If your child holds up one of her drawings, smiles, and says, 'Look at my drawing. Isn't it great?' you would empathically listen by saying something like, 'You're really proud of your drawing.' This gives her the message that it's okay to be proud of herself, and that can help build her self-esteem."

The therapist then teaches parents how to pace their empathic listening comments in such a way as to convey their genuine interest in the child without dominating or leading. Therapists can explain that content reflections of the child's play activities are similar to the play-by-play commentaries of sportscasters. In general, the therapist emphasizes the importance of identifying and reflecting the child's emotions in a brief, accurate, and natural-sounding manner. Parents also learn how to move about the room with the child in a way that does not intrude but shows their attentiveness.

Child-Centered Imaginary Play. Although many parents play with their children regularly, they sometimes do so in a rather directive manner, encouraging the child to play with certain toys or engage in play that is of educational value or of particular interest to the parents, for example, "Let's play this game. . . ." Other parents seldom play with their children or have difficulty engaging in pretend play for a variety of reasons. The child-centered imaginary play skill teaches parents how to act out various roles that the child might ask them to play and how to follow the child's lead while doing so.

Using an analogy of filmmaking can help parents understand their role in the child's imaginary play. The child is the actor-director of the play. The parent's role is that of an actor or actress under the child's direction who plays the part as the child determines. The child decides whether or not the parent gets a part, "writes the script" for that part, and indicates to the parent how to play it out. The therapist asks parents to avoid asking questions about their roles, as it can be difficult or distracting for children to put their play ideas into words. Instead, parents are asked to pay close attention to the child's verbal and nonverbal communications and to consider the context of the play when taking on a role as requested or directed. As parents master this skill, they become more sensitive to the child's (sometimes obscure) cues at the same time that they increase their comfort in engaging in imaginary play with the child. Parents need not use empathic listening skill while enacting an imaginary role, as that could be confusing for them. There is nothing inherently wrong with using both skills at once, but the key is to follow the child's lead. If the child has asked for a role to be played, parents learn to concentrate their efforts on that until the child's play shifts to something else. Through this more active form of empathic connection with their child, they are able to further the child's expression of thematic material in play.

Limit-Setting Skill. Many parents report that they have difficulty with the limit-setting skill. At the extremes are (a) parents who rarely, if ever, set enforceable limits; and (b) parents who do little else than set limits and enforce loud, harsh, or abusive consequences. Parents at both ends of this continuum often feel as though their children are the ones in control.

Between these extremes are parents who find consistency hard to attain – consistency between both parents as well as consistency from one day to the next. This can be a sensitive area for parents' self-esteem. The Filial therapist who reassures parents that he or she does not expect 100% consistency, but that consistency is an important goal, will probably get further in teaching and maximizing the parents' use of the limit-setting skill.

It is important that parents understand the need for skillful limit setting. Limit setting provides children with boundaries that are essential to their sense of security. Children are aware at some level that they are inexperienced and vulnerable, and when they see that they have control over their adult caretakers, their feelings of vulnerability can be increased. Also, when parents routinely threaten their children with consequences that they subsequently fail to carry out, they may be eroding the trust children place in them. Children may be learning that they cannot always believe what their parents say. Parents often have not thought of limit setting in these contexts. When a sensitive therapist covers these ideas with them, they frequently become eager to improve their skills.

In explaining the rationale of limit setting, the therapist also covers the following points:

1. Limit setting helps children learn that they are responsible for what happens to them if they choose to break a limit after having been previously warned of the consequences.
2. During play sessions, the parents keep limits to a minimum. This helps children remember them and fosters an atmosphere of freer expression of feelings.
3. When determining limits, it is important for parents to consider whether the limit is necessary for the child's safety, the safety of others, or the protection of valuable toys or property.
4. Limits need to be stated and enforced as consistently as possible so that the children learn that their parents "mean what they say." This helps reduce children's testing behaviors.

The Filial therapist initially teaches the limit-setting skill in simplified form as it relates to the play sessions. The same consequence is used for all broken limits during filial play sessions: After two chances to self-correct, if the child continues to break the stated limit, he or she must leave the playroom and the session is ended. This consequence quickly shows that parents are ultimately in charge and reestablishes eroded parental authority. The limits for the play sessions depend on the facility, but they often include:

1. The child should not throw anything at windows, mirrors, or cameras.
2. Crayons should not be used on the walls, furniture, or blackboards.
3. Sharp objects or hard-soled shoes should not be poked, thrown, or kicked at the bop bag.
4. The child may not leave the playroom except for one trip to the bathroom.
5. Dart guns should not be pointed or shot at people when they are loaded.

6. The child should not destroy valuable items or engage in mass destruction of toys.
7. Parents may need to set personal limits, but keep them to a minimum (e.g., no jumping on the parent's bad back; no dumping of an entire container of water on the parent).

The parents learn a three-step sequence of stating the limit, giving a warning, and enforcing the consequence for use during the play sessions.

Stating the Limit. When the child breaks or obviously is about to break one of the playroom limits, the parent states the limit to the child in a brief, clear, and specific manner. The tone of voice should be pleasant but firm and forceful. The parent uses the child's name, reflects the child's desire to engage in the prohibited behavior, then states the limit. After this the parent restructures, allowing the child to redirect his or her play. For example, "(Child's name), you'd like to shoot me with the gun. Remember I said I'd let you know if there's something you may not do? One of the things you may not do here is point or shoot the gun at me when it's loaded. But you may do almost anything else." The parent refrains from telling the child too specifically how or where to redirect the play and keeps the redirection statement quite general, permitting the child to solve the problem of how to redirect his or her energies and desires. This helps children learn to manage their impulses more responsibly. In cases where the broken limit is imminent, the parent may omit the empathic part of the statement, hold up his or her hand, and simply state the limit. If the child complies with the limit but complains about it, the parent returns to the use of empathic listening skill.

Giving a Warning. If the child breaks a limit the parent has already stated (i.e., the second time the behavior occurs in the session), the parent gives the child a warning. To do this, the parent restates the limit and then tells the child what will happen if the child breaks it again (i.e., leave the playroom). This allows the child to choose whether to risk the consequences. After the warning is given, the parent can restructure once again so the child can redirect his or her play. For example, "(Child's name), remember that I told you that you may not point or shoot the dart gun at me when it's loaded? If you point or shoot the loaded gun at me again, I will end the play time for today. You may do almost anything else."

Enforcing the Consequence. If the child breaks the limit for the third time that day, the parent must enforce the consequence of leaving the room. To do this, the parent restates the limit and then carries out the consequence given in the warning. A pleasant but firm tone of voice is used. The parent guides the child out of the room if necessary, similar to the process used with children resisting playroom departure at the end of a session. This procedure helps children learn that they are responsible for their own choices and behaviors and the outcomes associated with them. For example, "(Child's name), remember I told you if you pointed or shot the loaded dart gun at me we would leave the playroom? Since you chose to shoot it at me, we must leave. Right now." Parents also learn how to ignore tantrums that might occur after leaving the playroom in this manner.

If, in subsequent play sessions, the child breaks a limit that was stated in a previous play session, the parent proceeds from the second step of the limit-setting skill, reminding the child of the limit and warning the child of the consequence should the limit be broken again. For new infractions, the parent begins at the first step, stating the limit and redirecting the child's play.

THE FILIAL THERAPY TRAINING PROCESS

The Filial therapist teaches the skills to parents using a variety of training approaches, including brief lectures, demonstrations, modeling, role-playing, skills exercises, constructive feedback, and reinforcement. Between sessions, the therapist might ask parents to read portions of *A Parent's Handbook of Filial Therapy* (VanFleet, 2012a), which can augment their skills acquisition.

When first recommending Filial Therapy to parents, the therapist not only discusses the rationale for that recommendation but gives parents an overview of the play session and parenting skills they will learn. The therapist describes the four basic play session skills – structuring, empathic listening, child-centered imaginary play, and limit-setting – and discusses their importance in terms of the child's development and the family's reasons for seeking assistance. Following this discussion, the therapist trains the parents using a sequence of three phases: (a) play session demonstration, (b) initial skills training with the parents, and (c) mock play sessions for practice. Each of these training phases is described in the following sections. Video examples of the training process are available (VanFleet, 2006b, 2008).

Play Session Demonstration. In order to give parents a clearer picture of a Filial play session, the therapist conducts individual play sessions with each of the family's children (those who are 3 to 12 years old, approximately) while the parents observe. The observation is best accomplished through a one-way mirror, but parents may sit outside an open playroom door or observe from another room using remote electronic technologies. Parents can also observe from a corner of the playroom, if needed. In the latter case, the therapist coaches parents on remaining unobtrusive as they observe or record notes or questions for later discussion. Interestingly, an unexpected advantage of having parents observe from within the room has emerged. While playing with the therapist, children frequently look at their parents, show things to them, talk with them, or even ask their parents to play. The therapist continues the play session and helps parents stay in the observer role, but the children's desire for the parents' attention can later be discussed with the parents, showing them how important they are to their children, thus making a stronger case for their involvement in the play sessions.

The play session demonstrations usually require one full session. In families with more than one child, both parents ideally observe the play session demonstrations with each of their children, but this usually requires that the therapist arrange for some type of supervision of the children who are awaiting their turn for a play session. An alternative is for one parent to observe a play session demonstration while the other parent watches the remaining children, and then the parents switch roles as the therapist does a second demonstration with another child. Other variations may be necessary and are acceptable as long as each parent observes a play session with at least one of their own children.

Therapists may need to set limits and enforce consequences if a child breaks limits during the play session demonstrations, and they should inform parents of this possibility. Although the need to remove a child from the playroom happens rarely during play session demonstrations, everyone needs to be prepared for it. If the child becomes aggressive when leaving the playroom (e.g., hitting or kicking), the therapist can model for the parents an appropriate way to mildly restrain the child.

The therapist conducts brief child-centered play sessions, about 15 to 20 minutes in length, with each child. The therapist may shorten the time in families with more than two children. Following the demonstrations, the therapist meets with the parents alone to discuss their questions, concerns, and observations. If child supervision presents a problem, the therapist may postpone the bulk of the discussion until the next session, but some debriefing is important immediately after the demonstration.

The therapist invites parents to share their comments and questions, empathically listens to them, answers questions about the play sessions, and shares his or her own reactions to the play session. The therapist also points out whichever skills were demonstrated during the play sessions.

Initial Parent Training. The next phase of Filial Therapy involves the training of parents in the skills of structuring, empathic listening, child-centered imaginary play, and limit setting. The therapist describes the rationale and mechanics for each of the skills, giving examples whenever possible. The therapist may want to highlight the skills by referring back to examples of their use during the demonstration play session.

Using a few toys, the therapist plays briefly, giving each parent an opportunity to practice empathic listening. For example, the therapist can pile blocks higher and higher, simultaneously helping parents to give content reflections such as "You're putting another block on the pile . . . Another one . . . And now you're adding another . . . You're making a tall pile." The therapist then knocks the blocks down with an obvious look of joy and an expression such as "Whamo!" If the parents don't provide a reflection of the emotion expressed, the therapist can prompt them by saying, "How do you think I'm feeling?" The therapist helps them empathically listen to the feeling with something like, "It's fun to knock them all over . . . You like that!"

The therapist continues with such exercises until each parent is able to give basic content and feeling responses. After each try, the therapist gives the parents an opportunity to discuss how it felt to use the skill and to ask questions.

Principles of behavior and learning are relevant at this point. The therapist liberally uses positive reinforcement while giving feedback to the parents. The principle of shaping is very important as well. The therapist remains sensitive to the fact that parents are learning a new skill, and reinforces any steps in the right direction. Expectations of parents' performance of the skills need to be set just beyond their current levels of functioning.

Corrective feedback requires sensitivity as well. The therapist gives parents only one or two areas of skill refinement to focus on at a time. For example, the therapist might give a parent feedback in the following manner: "I really liked the way you said I (in my child role) was happy about knocking down the blocks. It was terrific that you picked up on my feelings like that! You seemed rather quiet while I was first piling up the blocks, so next time I'd like you to try to describe my actions aloud a bit more often. You definitely have the right idea; I'd just like to see you do a bit more of it. That will help children know that you're still paying attention and accepting their play. Do you have any questions or thoughts about this?"

Throughout the training process, whenever parents express their feelings and concerns, the therapist actively uses the empathic listening skill to convey understanding and acceptance of the parents and to model its use.

It is during this phase of training that the therapist not only covers the four basic skills but also discusses ways to handle negative reactions or questions the child may have during the play sessions. Parents learn to listen empathically to negative feelings the child expresses, such as when the child becomes angry after the parent has set a limit. The therapist emphasizes ways the parents can show acceptance of the feeling while standing firm in setting and enforcing the limit about the child's behavior. The therapist might model what to say when a child throws down a crayon after being told he or she may not use it on the walls: "You're mad that you can't color on the walls" or "You're mad I won't let you do that." Parents also learn that although they are accepting of the child's feelings of anger, they are to follow through firmly with the limit-setting procedure if the child attempts to write on the walls again.

Children sometimes ask questions when in the playroom, and the therapist teaches parents how to listen empathically to the intent of the question rather than automatically answering it. For example, if the child asks, "How many minutes left in the playroom?" the parent might respond, "You've been having a good time and don't want time to run out" or "You're wondering if there's much time left to play." If the child insists on an answer or seems unable to continue playing, then parents learn to give simple, nondirective answers. For example, if the child stops playing and continues, "Yes. How much more time?" the parent would respond, "There's quite a bit more time left. It's very important for you to be sure you have more time to be here. I'll let you know when it gets near the end." Giving the exact time is avoided, if possible, in order to preserve the nondirective atmosphere of the session and to prevent the child from becoming distracted by the time. If the child continues to insist on the exact time, the parent can give it, including a reflection of the underlying issue, the child's anxiety about not knowing the actual time or discomfort about not being in control of the play session time limits.

It is important for parents to learn to handle questions in this reflective, nondirective manner, especially when their child frequently looks to them for direction: "Mommy, can I play with this? Mommy, tell me how to use it." The therapist teaches parents to respond to the feelings and dynamics behind such requests, such as, "You want to know if it's okay for you to play with that. It's hard for you to decide on your own sometimes."

This initial training phase can usually be completed in one session.

Mock Play Sessions. In the next phase of the training process, parents individually practice conducting play sessions with the therapist playing the role of the child. Using the shaping principle, the therapist controls the degree of difficulty for the parents. Each parent's first mock play session lasts 10 or 15 minutes, and the Filial therapist usually plays a child who is reasonably straightforward and well-behaved.

The Filial therapist carefully chooses the content of the play during the mock session with several considerations in mind. First and foremost, the therapist plays in a manner that challenges parents to apply the skills but avoids overwhelming them. The degree of difficulty must be structured so that parents succeed on their first attempts. In other words, therapist expectations during the mock play sessions must be in line with parents' abilities.

Second, the therapist plays the child role in a manner that gives each parent practice in all major aspects of play sessions: entering the playroom; empathic listening to a variety of play styles, including mildly aggressive play; playing out a simple imaginary role as assigned by the child; handling at least one broken limit; giving 5- and 1-minute warnings; and leaving the playroom.

Third, the therapist selects some themes of play that are related to the family's presenting problems. Having previously observed and interacted with the children, the therapist usually has some idea of the children's likely behavior. For example, if one of the children plays quite aggressively and the parents' stated concerns include acting-out behaviors, the therapist would want to give the parents extra practice in limit setting during the mock play sessions. The therapist does not try to "be" one of the family's actual children, however, as that could be distracting from the skill acquisition focus of the training.

During the second mock play session, which also lasts 10 or 15 minutes, the Filial therapist increases the level of difficulty in accordance with the parents' growing proficiency with the skills. Skills that were weak during the first mock session require further practice, and the therapist makes certain parents are able to maintain their accepting attitudes even with more challenging child behaviors. The therapist also tests limits to a greater extent and gives parents more opportunities to engage in pretend play. The aim is to ensure that parents are able to handle most of the events common to play sessions in a manner consistent with child-centered play therapy principles. Two mock sessions usually are sufficient, but the therapist may want to hold more of them if parents have difficulty with any of the basic skills or concepts or if their children's presenting problems are particularly challenging or intense. For example, a third mock play session might be added for the adoptive parents of a child with serious attachment and conduct problems. The third session would focus more heavily on the use of the skills with very difficult child behaviors or intensely painful or trauma-related emotions.

Of great importance is the therapist's supervisory feedback to the parents during and after each mock play session. Individualized feedback is given to each parent. During the mock session, the therapist can step out of role briefly to give parents some immediate feedback. This can facilitate skill development and alleviate parents' performance anxieties. For example, the therapist might quickly say, "That was terrific! You picked up on my feelings of frustration very well" or "That's right – you need to set a limit when I'm pointing the loaded gun at you, but I'd like you to be more specific about what I may not do. Say something like, 'You may not point the gun at me when it's loaded.' Would you like to try again?" The therapist then returns immediately to the child role.

More extensive feedback is given after each mock play session. The Filial therapist gives parents an opportunity to discuss their reactions to the mock session and conveys acceptance and understanding of their feelings using empathic listening. The therapist then gives parents specific feedback about their use of the skills. Positive reinforcement should predominate. The therapist summarizes as specifically as possible the aspects that parents did well, such as, "Several times I noticed that you stopped yourself when you started to suggest that I play with another toy. It's tough to hold back from your usual way of interacting with children, but you did that beautifully." The therapist also suggests one or two areas for each parent to try to improve. For example, "Although you listened well when I expressed happy feelings, you seemed rather quiet when I was angrily punching the bop bag. That might give a child the idea that you disapprove of those angry feelings. Next time, I'd like you to try to reflect the negative or aggressive feelings a bit more. For example, when I was hitting the bop bag, you might have said something like 'You're really mad and you're putting that guy in his place.' Do you have any questions or concerns about this?" The therapist always shows acceptance of the parents' uncertainties about their own skills or the process prior to reassuring parents.

Parents are ready to begin supervised play sessions with their own children when they are able to remain in the empathic listening mode most of the time during mock play, are able to follow the therapist's (child's) lead in imaginary play, and are able to set specific limits using the three-step process. Parents' skills need not be "perfect" at this point, and the decision to move to the next phase is made jointly by the therapist and parents. The basic skills training period for Filial Therapy typically takes only a few sessions with an individual or couple and about 2 months with Filial Therapy groups of six to eight parents (L. F. Guerney & B. G. Guerney, 1987).

COMMON PROBLEMS IN THE TRAINING PHASE

The most common problems during the training phase of Filial Therapy involve difficulties with skill acquisition, parents' impatience with the delays in addressing some of their children's problems, and parents' uncertainties about their own abilities or about Filial Therapy. The therapist handles all of these with a great deal of acceptance and patience.

During skill acquisition, parents often struggle to refrain from directing children's play, have difficulty identifying children's feelings, have trouble playing imaginatively, or are ineffective in setting and enforcing limits. A mixture of parent practice, therapist empathy, specific reinforcement, suggestions for improvement, and encouragement to try again usually helps parents master the skills. A lighthearted atmosphere during the mock play training sessions also facilitates learning.

Many times parents come to therapy expecting rapid solutions to their children's problems. Although some problems can be remedied in a very short period, more complex problems cannot. Filial Therapy does not offer a quick fix. Filial therapists encourage parents to voice their frustrations about delays in addressing problems, listen carefully to them, and patiently explain that problems that have existed for months or years usually cannot be eliminated overnight. This is especially true for problems with emotional roots. Therapists can help reduce some of this pressure by suggesting behavioral interventions, but they need to emphasize the longer term benefits that are possible when parents learn new skills and ways of interacting with their children.

Therapists can handle parents' uncertainties about their own abilities to learn by showing understanding of the parents' feelings and helping them put the learning process in perspective. Analogies to other types of skill development can help. Most parents remember the awkwardness they felt when first learning to drive a car, a skill most people do without thinking once they learn it. Learning new parenting skills follows the same sequence, becoming more automatic with practice.

Parents' doubts about the Filial Therapy process must be dealt with openly. Again, therapists need to listen carefully and refrain from defensive reactions. When parents believe that the therapist truly understands their concerns, they are usually willing to listen to further explanations of the potential benefits Filial Therapy offers them.

CASE STUDY

During the play session demonstration, Jessi played with a variety of toys, but concentrated on the bop bag and the dart guns. Her play was quite active throughout. She tried to shoot the dart gun at me (the therapist), but she responded well when I set the limit. During his play session, Josh exhibited exploratory play and seemed to enjoy the kitchen area and talking on the telephones with me. I was able to demonstrate all four of the basic skills, structuring and empathically listening with both children, imaginary play with Josh on the phones, and limit setting with Jessi and the dart guns. Carol and Ed were able to watch both sessions. As we discussed the skills and the children's play, I noted that Jessi had not tried to test the limits after I told her she could not point the dart gun at me when it was loaded. Both parents were interested in the process, and we agreed to continue with the training phase.

During the mock play sessions, Ed followed me around the room well and reflected my feelings accurately. He was rather quiet most of the time. I was able to reinforce his ability to empathically listen to my emotions, and I suggested that he simply try to do it more often. He seemed encouraged and did better during his second mock session.

Carol was able to reflect positive feelings which I expressed, and she followed my lead very well during imaginary play. She had difficulty, however, when I expressed aggressive or negative emotions. When I was hitting the bop bag very hard and when I played aggressively with the doll family, she watched but said nothing. I pointed the loaded dart gun at her, and she said, "You can't do that!"

She expressed her discomfort with the aggressive play when we discussed the mock session afterward. As she thought about having play sessions with Jessi, she worried that the aggressive toys and the empathic listening would stimulate rather than eliminate Jessi's bad behaviors. After listening carefully to her concerns, I explained that we might see an increase in Jessi's aggressive play in the play sessions, but it would most likely decrease as she worked through her issues and as Carol and Ed became more confident with their limit setting. We also spent some time discussing the nature of aggression. I stressed that emotions – positive and negative – are part of all of us, and the key is to learn to express them appropriately with our words and behavior. The play sessions would provide a safe, contained environment in which Jessi could learn to do that. Carol seemed satisfied with this explanation.

When giving Carol feedback about her skills, I was able to reinforce her imaginary play and her reflection of my positive feelings. I also reinforced the way she held back from correcting me when I was playing aggressively. I gave her a few examples of how she could have reflected my negative feelings. I also reinforced her quickness and tone of voice when setting the limit with me but indicated that she needed to be more specific about what I could not do. We practiced limit setting on a few more examples. She improved a great deal during her second mock play session, although she remained a bit hesitant with her empathic listening in aggression situations.

The training period for the Taylors, including the play session demonstrations, initial training, and two mock sessions each for Ed and Carol, took four 1-hour meetings.

PARENTS' INITIAL PLAY SESSIONS

PREPARING PARENTS

When the training phase has been completed, Filial therapists prepare parents for their first play sessions with their children. The therapist answers any final questions the parents might have and then discusses what the parents might expect from the child during their play sessions. If the child has played aggressively during the family play observation or the play session demonstration, the therapist would want to make certain the parents understand how to listen empathically to aggressive themes and also how to set limits effectively. Although some potential behaviors are discussed, the therapist indicates that there is really no way to predict how children will react to the play sessions with their parents. Parents are told that if they run into trouble during their first play sessions, they always have the option of giving the 5-minute warning early and then ending the session. Therapists can also reassure parents that they will be observing and can step in if absolutely needed. The therapist should also highlight the skill levels developed by the parents during the training sessions to encourage them and to show confidence in them.

SUPERVISING INITIAL PLAY SESSIONS

The first play sessions that parents hold with their children are for 20 minutes; all subsequent play sessions are 30 minutes long. One parent plays with one child at a time to permit individualized attention. When possible, parents conduct play sessions with each of their children under the therapist's supervision. The therapist observes the play sessions and gives supervisory feedback to the parents afterward. If possible, the parents observe each other's play sessions as well. A one-way mirror is ideal for observation. If this arrangement is unavailable, the therapist and the other parent can observe from a position just outside the open playroom door. The least preferred method is for the therapist and parent to observe from within the playroom, in a corner that is marked by furniture arrangement or other means as being distinct from the rest of the playroom. When the therapist and the other parent are visible to the parent and child having a play session, they must take care to be as unobtrusive as possible during the observations. The appearance that they are watching the child and then writing down those observations must be avoided. Use of peripheral vision while observing can be helpful. Electronic and wireless technology advances are broadening the options for unobtrusive or remote observation of the parent-child play sessions.

Filial therapists watch for several things during the initial parent-child play sessions. They observe the parent's use of the play session skills – both effective use of the skills and areas that need improvement. Although the observations during these initial sessions focus primarily on each parent's skill development, therapists also note any themes that emerge in the child's play. At this stage, themes can often be identified by the intensity of the child's play or by play that is quite repetitious or focused.

Some Filial therapists have found it helpful to record observation notes in the format shown in the following example. Therapist reactions are shown in the third column.

Child Behavior	Parent Behavior	Comments
Walked around room looking things over.	"You're checking this place out."	Good!
Punched bop bag several times, harder each time; watched for mom's reaction.	Said nothing.	Discuss Parent's feelings; need to listen empathically.
Shot dart gun at light.	"You like shooting that gun."	Great! Reflected the child's expression and feeling.
Shot gun from farther and farther away.	"You're still shooting."	Still describing the behavior – Good! Maybe add, "You're to see if you can hit the light from farther away."
"You can't shoot as good as I can!"	Said nothing.	Discuss possible listening responses: "You like to beat me" or "You're proud of your shooting."
		Overall great job! Really letting the child lead!

Following the play session, the therapist discusses it in detail with the parent who conducted it. The therapist includes the other parent who observed the play session in the feedback discussion but does not permit him or her to offer advice or criticism. The therapist first elicits and empathically listens to the parent's reaction to the play session. It can benefit the learning process when parents have the opportunity to critique their behavior in the playroom first and to discuss their reactions to the child's play and the process. The therapist then offers specific skill feedback: reinforcement for times when the parent used the skills effectively and suggestions for improvement in one or two areas. Reference to specific events or comments during the play session is important. Care is taken not to overwhelm the parent with feedback. The observing parent is invited to ask questions about the play session after the therapist feedback is completed. Giving parents a copy of the therapist's process notes can strengthen the open and collaborative nature of the therapist-parent relationship.

After the skill feedback, discussion turns to the nature of the child's play during the session. Filial therapists gradually help parents gain greater understanding of the symbolism and possible meanings of their children's play. Therapists with different theoretical orientations might interpret the play's symbolism differently, and various schools of thought could be integrated with Filial Therapy. Given the psycho-educational basis of Filial Therapy and the parents' level of understanding of psychological principles, however, most Filial therapists make interpretations that stay relatively close to the child's play behavior. For example, they look for themes of control, security, peer or family relationships, mastery, self-esteem, and other developmental issues that might reflect how the child is reacting to his or her present situation.

At this early stage, the therapist invites parents to voice their concerns and questions about the child's play. After full discussion of parent issues, the therapist points out other play themes which seem to be emerging and asks parents whether they have noticed those themes in other aspects of the child's life. For example, if the child tends to ignore the parent when limits are set during play sessions, the therapist would inquire whether the parents have noticed similar "hearing problems" at home. Provided that actual auditory problems have been ruled out, the therapist discusses with parents their usual way of handling such incidents and helps them enforce consequences more effectively.

When Filial therapists discuss play themes with parents, they also inform parents about the factors that led them to recognize the themes.

Usually these factors include the intensity or focus of the child's play, the frequency with which the child plays with particular items, or the enactment of similar sequences of behavior. If a boy who is small for his age and subject to teasing from his peers frequently pretends he is a large and powerful monster, giant, or superhero, the therapist might suggest to the parents that the theme represents his desire and attempt to have greater control over his life.

Usually only two or three initial play sessions are needed for skill refinement. Children often use the early sessions in an exploratory fashion, discovering the toys available in the playroom and becoming familiar with the way the play sessions work. Strong thematic play often emerges after these initial sessions when parents and children alike have developed a "feel" for the play sessions.

COMMON PROBLEMS DURING INITIAL PLAY SESSIONS

Problems at this stage of Filial Therapy are similar to those encountered during the training phase, and the therapist handles them in the same manner. In addition, conducting play sessions with their children can evoke parental concerns or fears about the meaning of their children's play. It is not uncommon for parents to wonder if their child might someday be a delinquent because of a great interest in the dart guns or to express concerns about their son's gender identity if he plays with dolls.

Filial therapists take all parent questions seriously and show non-judgmental acceptance of their feelings. Therapists at this stage often find themselves reassuring parents that their child's behavior is not cause for concern and is often functional. Aggressive play is natural, especially during early play sessions, and the skills parents are learning throughout Filial Therapy will help parents rear healthy, responsible children. And boys will play with dolls as eagerly as girls, if given the opportunity. In essence, there's a tendency for parents to read too much into their children's play when they first learn about symbolism, and Filial therapists help parents keep their interpretations in perspective. In addition, the therapist warns the parents that there must be no questioning or repercussions regarding the child's play outside the session and encourages them to continue to raise their concerns during their meetings with the therapist.

CASE STUDY

Ed seemed more relaxed in his first play session with Jessi. Her play was exploratory without much expression of feeling. He gave good content reflections and did well the one time Jessi placed him in a role at a "tea party." He forgot to give the 5-minute warning, but remembered the 1-minute warning. He indicated afterward that it had been much easier for him with a child; he didn't feel as self-conscious. He was pleased with his performance. I agreed with him and suggested that he continue to try to increase the frequency of his empathic listening comments.

Carol's first play session with Josh also went smoothly. He explored the playroom at first and then played with the kitchen set. Carol's use of empathic listening was excellent. When Josh spilled some water on the floor, she quickly jumped up to mop it up with some napkins, but returned to her nondirective role right away. Josh also pretended he was Batman and punched his enemies (the bop bag), but he did not involve Carol in his imaginary play. Carol was happy with the way the play session had gone. I praised the many things she had done well, and then we discussed her reaction to the spilled water. She said she was so used to cleaning up after Josh that she hadn't realized what she had done until it was over. She readily understood how her reaction could convey nonacceptance in the play session context.

Ed's next session was with Josh. Josh explored the room some more and then played Batman for the last half of the session. He asked Ed to play the Joker. Ed had some difficulty getting into the "bad guy" role, and Josh became a little frustrated because Ed wasn't "mean enough." After we talked about the things that had gone well, we discussed Ed's feelings about the role he had been given. He said he had grown up on a farm and didn't remember having much time for imaginary play when he was a boy. We practiced making ugly faces and using menacing voices, and he said he would try that the next time it was asked for.

Jessi's play was quite different with Carol. She played with the bop bag and the dart guns much of the time. She tried to shoot Carol twice with the dart gun, and Carol set the limit and then gave the warning as she should, although she forgot to redirect Jessi's play. When Carol told Jessi it was time to leave the playroom, Jessi began putting some of the kitchen dishes away. Carol reminded her it was time to go, but allowed her to finish cleaning up.

During the feedback portion of the session, Carol expressed concern that Jessi had "played better" with Ed the week before. She felt hurt that

Jessi seemed to test her much more. She acknowledged that Ed might be right, that there was a power struggle between Jessi and her. I reassured her that this did not mean she was a "bad mother" and reminded her that one of our purposes in using Filial Therapy was to strengthen their relationship. When discussing the skills, I complimented Carol on her ability to refrain from directing Jessi's play, her use of the listening skill in general, and her firm limit setting. I also pointed out to her that Jessi had not tested the limit a third time.

Carol was surprised when I suggested that in the future she try to get Jessi to leave the room right away at the end, even if she wanted to put her toys away. She had been pleased at Jessi's willingness to clean up when that was usually a battle at home. I indicated that some children use cleaning up at the very end of the play session as a delay tactic, perhaps another way of testing the limits. I also clarified that they needn't clean the room – that was one of the things that kept the play sessions special and avoided possible limit testing at the end.

These initial play sessions were completed in two meetings.

CONTINUING PLAY SESSIONS
UNDER DIRECT SUPERVISION

As parents become more proficient in the conduct of play sessions with their children, the Filial therapist's focus gradually shifts from skill development to therapeutic issues. The therapist always remains aware of parents' use of the skills and continues to provide reinforcement and corrective feedback but spends an increasing proportion of time attending to child and family dynamics. The supervisory process follows the same format for all play sessions done under the therapist's direct supervision. At the end of each, the therapist elicits and empathically listens to the parent's reactions, reinforces specific things the parent did well, suggests one or two areas for improvement in the next session, and then discusses the themes in the child's play.

THEMATIC PLAY

By the third or fourth Filial play session, themes have usually begun to emerge in the children's play. Children typically exhibit exploratory play during the first session or two, although therapeutically significant themes are possible that early. As children gain a sense of the permissive, nonjudgmental atmosphere of the play sessions, they begin to express some of their deeper feelings and conflicts through their play. Play themes often relate to real-life issues, and they sometimes carry over from one session to the next. Themes of aggression, nurturance, mastery, control, power and authority, good and evil, family relationships, and peer relationships are common. Children also express many developmental processes during play sessions. The toys and methods through which children express these themes in their play seem limitless.

Children, especially those with aggression problems and those from homes that have repressed the expression of anger, often display aggressive themes during this stage of therapy. Use of the dart guns, bop bag, knife, or rope is common, and the play can be very active. Limit-testing behaviors may also increase. Parents sometimes voice a concern that Filial Therapy is opening Pandora's box, exacerbating the children's problems rather than alleviating them. Filial therapists need to explain that this rise in aggressive play is common and temporary. The goal of Filial Therapy is to help children learn constructive ways of dealing with aggression, and aggressive play usually gives way to other themes once children work through their issues.

Interpreting the meanings of children's play must take into account the context of the child's and family's life (VanFleet et al., 2010). Interpretations of play choices or themes that rely on "cookbook" approaches (e.g., dinosaurs = aggression; baby dolls = nurturance) without consideration of context are bound to be inaccurate or incomplete. Children's repetitiveness, intensity, and other behaviors provide clues about what their play means to them, but the filial therapist is always mindful of the broader happenings in the child's life, past and present, and uses them to place the play in context. The parents are true partners here as they know more about that context than anyone other than the child.

The meaning of children's play is not always clear. Filial therapists help parents form "hypotheses" about possible meanings of the play and help parents have patience while the thematic patterns emerge more clearly over several play sessions. Furthermore, Filial therapists help parents accept that it is not necessary for them to understand everything about their children's play themes in order for the play sessions to have therapeutic impact. (For an extensive discussion of play themes in nondirective play sessions, see VanFleet et al., 2010).

DEALING WITH DYNAMIC ISSUES

The focus on children's play themes invariably leads to discussion of dynamic issues within the family. The children's behavior in the playroom raises questions for parents about the children and about themselves.

Children's Issues. "Is that normal?" is a question parents frequently ask during this stage of therapy. They have begun to see their children's play in a new light, but their inexperience with the symbolism of play sometimes causes them to worry, usually unnecessarily, about the "normality" of their children's play. Until parents become better at understanding the meaning of their children's play, the filial therapist reassures them and reframes the play to aid their understanding of it. For example, after a play session in which a young girl pummels the bop bag at length, her parents might wonder if this is a sign that she's really a violent person whose expressions of anger must be even more tightly controlled. The therapist needs to elicit these concerns and reassure the parents that such aggressive play is natural for both boys and girls and to be expected at this point in therapy. Further explanation about the role of anger and aggression in human life might be warranted. The therapist can extend the discussion to include ways for the parents to encourage more appropriate expression of anger at home.

Filial therapists help parents avoid reading too much into their children's play while teaching them to understand its meaning for the children. This is accomplished by discussion of parents' reactions, reframing, and therapist modeling. Because it is easy for parents to misinterpret their children's play at this point, it is vital that Filial therapists remain alert for and encourage open discussion of parental concerns about their children's play session behavior.

Parents' Issues. Closely related to parents' questions about their children's behavior are their concerns about their own competence as parents. As they strive to understand the meaning of their children's play, parents frequently wonder what that play implies about them as parents. Discussion of these issues can provide the driving force for change in the family or it can threaten the family's participation in therapy.

It is essential that Filial therapists remain sensitive to parents' feelings about themselves as reflected by the play sessions. When a mother sees her 4-year-old son pick up the mother doll and fly her through the air on a make-believe broomstick, all the while cackling and casting evil spells on the family dolls below, she might worry that her son perceives her as a witch. She might very well feel threatened by the Filial Therapy process that has revealed this to her and begin to have doubts about further involvement. Vigilant therapists will recognize such play as potentially threatening to parents and will raise it for thorough discussion if parents do not.

The context of the children's play is extremely important for these discussions. The interpretation of the witch play might be different if Halloween is nearing and the mother doll is the closest approximation of a witch in the playroom than if the mother has reported that she constantly punishes her son for his endless misdeeds at home. Filial therapists listen to parents' concerns and then explore with them a variety of possible explanations for the play. Extreme caution is exercised in drawing conclusions from a single play sequence.

There are times when Filial therapists' interpretations of children's play might reflect negatively on the parents. When this is the case, therapists need to help parents understand the implications of the play while at the same time reducing parents' defensiveness. If parents become defensive about the play or its interpretation, they are unlikely to hear what the therapist has to say or to change their behavior.

To reduce defensiveness, therapists can use empathic listening to convey acceptance of the parent while reframing the problem in terms of the parents' feelings. Therapists can also reinforce parents for recognizing and facing negative interpretations and for their involvement in therapy that has permitted this new understanding of the child. At no time does the therapist suggest that they are bad parents. The focus needs to be on the parents' feelings and behavior and possible ways to change the situation.

For example, if the therapist agrees from the context of the child's play that the boy really does see his mother as a punitive witch, the therapist might say to the mother, "You're upset that your son thinks of you as a witch. It hurts that he doesn't seem to recognize all the nice things you do for him" (empathic listening). "Although we don't know for certain if this is what his play means, let's take a minute to talk about that possibility. Even though it's painful right now, I think you've already laid the groundwork to solve this problem. Because you've done such a great job creating an open atmosphere in the playroom, he feels free to express his feelings, and we're now in a better position to improve your relationship with him because we have some idea how he feels. During the intake, you told me that you were very frustrated with his behavior and had to be after him all the time. It seems to me that you were already aware of this problem, and you took steps to get help. I really believe that we can reduce your frustration with his bad behavior and his possible perception of you as a witch. Why don't you tell me more about your feelings on this, and then we can talk further about how to deal with this problem."

In this example, the therapist empathically listens to the mother's concerns, reframes the problem in terms of the mother's frustration, sincerely reinforces her efforts so far, and then offers hope that the problem can be resolved. The son's revelation, when handled in a sensitive manner, can help motivate the mother to try new ideas in her relationship with her son. The therapist might then highlight the value of the positive attention the mother gives her son in the playroom and the importance of the limit-setting skill for consistent discipline in addressing both her frustration with his behavior and her "witch image."

In summary, dynamic issues are generated through children's thematic play, interactions between parent and child in the playroom, and parents' reactions to them. It is the complex interplay of the skills training and the discussion of dynamic issues that provides the tools and the momentum for family change, and it is during this phase of Filial Therapy that this usually begins to occur. The therapist continues direct supervision of parents conducting play sessions until a solid foundation has been built, in terms both of the parents' play session skills and the parents' ability to recognize and openly discuss their children's play themes.

Families vary considerably in the length of time that they require direct therapist supervision of the play sessions. Filial therapists typically observe at least five or six actual parent play sessions between the training period and the start of home play sessions. Only when parents have become competent and confident in conducting play sessions does the therapist show them how to transfer the play sessions to the home setting.

COMMON PROBLEMS DURING
LATER SUPERVISED PLAY SESSIONS

Problems at this stage of Filial Therapy center on the logistics of having the parents hold play sessions with each of their children while maintaining the relatively short-term focus of Filial Therapy. Filial

Therapy seems to work best when each of the parents (or grandparents or other caregivers) holds play sessions with each of the children in the family. From the therapist's viewpoint, the parents can learn to hold play sessions quite readily by "practicing" with different children, and this may even enhance the learning process. Parents are challenged in different ways by playing with each of their children and seem to learn the skills more quickly. Furthermore, the family therapy nature of the intervention is preserved. Nevertheless, with several children this can pose a problem in scheduling the sessions in a time-efficient manner.

When using a 1-hour therapy format, two options are possible. During the supervised play sessions, parents can alternate their play sessions from week to week and from child to child. Each week one parent holds a 25- to 30-minute play session with a child while the therapist and other parent observe. The therapist then meets with both parents to provide feedback and discuss the session. The next week, the other parent holds a play session with another of the children. This alternation of weeks and children continues until the therapist has observed each parent five or six times.

The second option works best if sessions can be extended to 75 minutes, but it can be done within 60 minutes if necessary. In this format, one parent holds a play session with one child for 20 minutes while the therapist and other parent observe. Ten minutes are used for the feedback process involving both parents and to reset the room for the next play session. Then the other parent holds a play session for 20 minutes, with the final 10 minutes for that feedback process. The recommended extra 15 minutes permits time for discussion of other issues that have arisen at home and for scheduling the next visit.

Although the logistics of supervising several different parent-child combinations for play sessions seems daunting, they usually work themselves out rather easily. The value of providing this degree of follow-through and support for the family far outweighs the inconveniences that scheduling sometimes poses. Parents usually are eager to hold the play sessions by this point in therapy, and the problems are readily resolved.

CASE STUDY

I supervised the Taylors' play sessions three more times, for a total of five sessions per parent, before they began to conduct home sessions.

Their skills continued to develop, and the children's play themes became more pronounced.

During the latter three meetings, Carol held two play sessions with Jessi and one with Josh while Ed conducted two with Josh and one with Jessi. Josh seemed to enjoy playing with the kitchen set, pouring water back and forth in the dishes. He continued with his superhero play, primarily Batman. Ed succeeded at being a "meaner, trickier" Joker as Josh wanted. Josh thoroughly enjoyed the play sessions, and he engaged Ed more and more with his imaginary play. His play with Carol was similar. He used the bop bag as the Joker and other villains instead of Carol, but he involved her in some puppet play. Josh used what he called the "dragon" puppet to playfully attack Carol's puppets. Josh's play themes seemed to reflect both mastery and control issues, and none of them appeared unusual.

Jessi's aggressive play became more pronounced during these sessions. She tested Ed once by throwing a toy at him. He hesitantly set the limit, "I don't think you can do that." She did not press further. With Ed, she played card games which she invariably won, and Ed did a good job reflecting her desire to beat him. She also continued playing with the dart gun and bop bag. Her aggression was more apparent with Carol. Although Carol never had to end a play session, Jessi began testing a number of limits. She tried shooting the dart gun at her again, she threw a toy in Carol's direction, and she tried to poke the bop bag with one of the hard plastic forks from the kitchen set. Each time, she glanced at Carol, watching for her reaction. Carol set the limits well. After Carol stated the limit, Jessi tossed aside the toy she had been using and grumbled about how "This place is no fun. Just like home." Carol had some difficulty reflecting Jessi's feelings at those times. Jessi again tried to clean the room at the end of the session, and Carol handled that well. Jessi did not test Carol as much during their third play session together; she played by herself most of the time while Carol reflected.

We did some work refining Ed's and Carol's skills, particularly Ed's need to set limits more specifically and firmly and Carol's need to reflect angry feelings. After we discussed their use of the skills each time, we talked about the children's play themes. They both readily understood Josh's play, but they expressed concern about Jessi's. They needed further reassurance that her increase in aggression was part of the process and that it would not remain forever. They did not report any increase in her "bad behavior" at home. Both of them indicated that they were feeling more comfortable in the playroom, and I could see great improvement in both of them.

After these three additional meetings, we all felt confident moving the play sessions to the home setting. We scheduled our next meeting to discuss the transfer of the play sessions.

THE TRANSFER OF PLAY
SESSIONS TO THE HOME SETTING

Planning for the transfer of the play sessions to the home setting can begin early in Filial Therapy. During the training phase, the therapist gives parents a list of the toys they will need to acquire for the home play sessions. The therapist reminds parents of the need to gather toys when they begin their play sessions under the therapist's supervision. When parents are ready to transfer the sessions, the Filial therapist spends one full session helping them prepare for it. Planning consider-ations include acquiring the toys, deciding where play sessions will be held, scheduling the play sessions, handling interruptions, committing the necessary time for the play sessions, and watching for changes in the children's play.

ACQUISITION OF TOYS

The therapist encourages parents to obtain a set of toys which they will keep separate from the children's other toys and use only during their Filial play sessions. The listing of toys described earlier (pp. 24-25) is used as a guide. The cost of purchasing a basic toy kit is ap-proximately $150 to $200.

Many families cannot afford to buy an entirely new set of toys, so the therapist works with them to identify economical ways to furnish their playrooms. For example, a cardboard box with dividers inside can substitute for a dollhouse. Animal families sometimes are less expensive than human doll families, and children tend to use them just as readily to express family themes. Someone in the family might be able to make a puppet family using socks for the bodies, marking pens or buttons for the facial features, and yarn for the hair. Different-sized plastic bowls from butter or margarine containers can serve as kitchen dishes, and a one-quart plastic milk or juice bottle works well as the water container. As long as the therapist remembers the basic principles for creating a child-centered play environment, innovations are bounded only by the therapist's and family's creativity. Flea markets and yard sales can be sources of inexpensive toys. Therapists who have posted a list of needed items at their workplaces often receive useful donations from coworkers. Some Filial therapists have loaned sets of toys to indigent families, and small grants may be available from charitable groups for the purchase of Filial toy sets.

LOCATION FOR PLAY
SESSIONS IN THE HOME

The therapist also works with the parents to determine the best location in their home for the play sessions. The location need not remain set up as a playroom between sessions – parents can store the toys in a closet when not in use. There are several considerations when selecting a location: (a) The space needs to be large and open enough to permit bop bag play, two people, and the rest of the toys (8' x 10' or larger, if possible), (b) it should be cleared of breakable and valuable items, (c) it needs to withstand some rough-and-tumble play without the need for many additional limits, and (d) it should be suitable for water play and spills. Common choices include kitchens, basement rooms, and garages. Smaller spaces marked off within a larger room are acceptable. Creativity may be required for families who reside in small mobile homes or apartments. In very limited spaces, placing a sheet or blanket on the floor to delineate the "play space" and placing the toys on top of that can work quite well.

After a suitable location is designated, the therapist works with the parents to determine what additional limits might be necessary. The number of limits needs to be kept to a minimum in order to preserve the permissive atmosphere of the play sessions, but some tailoring to the home setting is usually necessary.

SCHEDULE OF PLAY SESSIONS

The therapist recommends that each parent schedule a half-hour play session with each child per week. Modifications to this plan are sometimes necessary for families with several children or when families have custody, visitation, or out-of-town work schedule constraints. It is of prime importance that play sessions be regular and predictable from the children's point of view and probably should be held at least biweekly for gains to be derived. Because parents have been conducting play sessions on a regular basis under the therapist's supervision, many scheduling problems may have already been worked out. The therapist emphasizes the need to continue with regularity at home.

The parents need to keep the children's interests and activities in mind when scheduling the home Filial sessions. Play sessions that compete with favorite television shows, soccer practices, or prime neighborhood play times are not likely to be successful.

HANDLING INTERRUPTIONS

Interruptions have the potential to destroy the special nature and momentum of play sessions, and interruptions are likely to happen in the home setting. Therefore, the therapist encourages parents to anticipate the types of interruptions they might encounter and to decide in advance how they will handle them. Parents can inform friends and neighbors when they will be unavailable in order to discourage unannounced visitors during the Filial sessions, and answering machines or removal of the receiver from the hook can prevent disrupting telephone calls. Mobile phones are best left in another room and turned off.

Siblings can account for many potential interruptions. In two-parent households, the other parent can keep the remaining children occupied, but this presents a challenge for single parents or those with partners who are unwilling or unable to help. Enlisting the aid of older siblings, relatives, or neighbors might be necessary. Sometimes conducting play sessions that take advantage of school schedules can work well. Such logistics problems can usually be worked out, but they require creative thought.

COMMITMENT

Prior to starting home sessions, parents have been involved in Filial Therapy for approximately 10 weeks (beyond the assessment) and have a significant investment in the process. It is important for that commitment to continue as they move the play sessions to home. The commitment is to their children and to their relationships with them. Filial therapists emphasize the clinical importance of regular, uninterrupted play sessions at home. In essence, the parents must show the children that when they are having their play sessions, the children are the top priority for the parents. Parents need to communicate that nothing is more important to them than their children during the play sessions, and this is best communicated by their commitment and follow-through in holding the play sessions as planned. If something unexpected interferes with a planned play session, the parent needs to inform the child in advance and reschedule it.

CHANGES IN CHILDREN'S PLAY

A final preparation for home play sessions involves possible changes in children's behavior in the play sessions. The therapist informs the parents that changes might be noted in the children's play due to the change in environment. Sometimes there is an initial increase in limit testing by the children during Filial sessions at home. Sometimes the focus of their play themes changes. Usually the changes are minor and are easily handled by parents, but it is helpful for parents to know in advance that they might occur so they won't worry unnecessarily if they do.

HOME PLAY SESSIONS AND
GENERALIZATION OF SKILLS

As parents conduct play sessions at home with their children, a new phase of Filial Therapy begins. It focuses on (a) maintenance of parents' play skills during the sessions, (b) continuing discussion of child and parent issues, (c) monitoring of progress being made toward therapeutic goals, (d) use of play session skills in the broader context of family life, and (e) learning and application of additional parenting skills.

THERAPIST SUPERVISION
OF HOME PLAY SESSIONS

The Filial therapist meets with the parents weekly or biweekly, but at least after every two home play sessions that each parent conducts. For each play session, the therapist asks the parents to complete a self-supervision questionnaire that becomes the basis for discussion. The questionnaire contains four open-ended questions:

1. What aspects of this play session did I handle well?
2. What aspects of this play session might have been improved?
3. What were the primary themes of the child's play?
4. What questions did this play session raise for me about Filial Therapy, my skills, my child, my family, or me?

The therapist thoroughly discusses the play sessions with the parents as before. Together they cover strengths and weaknesses in the use of the play skills, questions about the way certain child behaviors were handled, and play themes and their possible meanings. Much attention continues to focus on the dynamic issues raised by the play themes and subsequent problem solving.

If the parents report significant new problems in the conduct of the home sessions or if therapists fear the erosion of parents' play session skills, therapists can request that the parents bring their children in for direct supervision of a play session. When families' problems are extensive, it is a good idea for the therapist to directly supervise play sessions as a matter of course. Depending on the nature of the problems, the therapist might ask to watch a live session every 6 or 8 weeks to ensure maintenance of the child-centered approach.

GENERALIZATION OF PLAY SESSION SKILLS

After home play sessions are underway, the therapist devotes part of every therapy session to the generalization of play session skills. It is not unusual for parents to ask how they might apply empathic listening or limit setting outside play sessions. The motivation that parents develop as a result of their successes using the skills in the playroom makes the therapist's job relatively easy at this point.

Filial therapists now encourage parents to listen empathically to their children in a wide range of daily situations. Specific situations are suggested for practice – when the children talk about their day at school; when children feel hurt, disappointed, or angry with someone else or with the parents; when the children feel proud of themselves – but parents are encouraged to try the listening skill any time they think of it. The therapist can give homework assignments to listen empathically several times during the week and report back on the results.

The therapist also helps parents apply the three-step limit-setting procedure to behavior problems outside the play sessions. This involves deciding what the limits need to be, how to state them specifically and clearly, and what realistic, enforceable consequences can be applied as consistently as possible. Homework assignments that require parents to plan how they could use the limit-setting skill in new situations can facilitate its generalization.

ADDITIONAL PARENTING SKILLS

At this phase of therapy, the therapist also introduces several additional parenting skills to the parents: setting realistic expectations, parent messages, a broader application of structuring, and reinforcement. The realistic expectations skill emphasizes parents' use of child development and readiness information in deciding what they should expect of their children at different stages. The parent messages skill helps parents communicate their needs and wishes to their children more clearly and straightforwardly. The expanded structuring skill focuses on ways parents can anticipate and reduce obstacles to their children's problem solving and how to "set their children up for success." The reinforcement skill covers the use of positive reinforcement and behavior management approaches which are usually much more effective than punishment.

The therapist helps parents generalize their play session skills and teaches them additional parenting skills by discussing the rationale for each skill, demonstrating its use, supervising parent practice of the skill, and assigning homework exercises. L. F. Guerney's books, *Parenting: A Skills Training Manual* (1995) and *A Clinician's and Group Leader's Manual for Parenting: A Skills Training Program* (1987), are useful references for parents and therapists. The lessons described in the leader's manual work very well with the Filial Therapy model, and the training manual can be used for homework reading and exercises for the parents.

COMMON PROBLEMS
DURING HOME PLAY SESSIONS

Two different categories of problems occur at this phase: problems implementing the play sessions at home and concerns about the child's play themes or other therapeutic issues.

Problems Implementing Home Play Sessions. Even when filial therapists have thoroughly prepared parents for the home play sessions, some of the anticipated obstacles still occur. Most common are interruptions during the play sessions, scheduling conflicts, and declines in the parents' use of the play session skills. Therapists handle the interruption and scheduling problems in much the same way that they helped parents prepare for them. They discuss the family's lifestyle and the obstacles they have encountered and then work jointly with the family to explore other options or approaches. A certain degree of patience and creativity can help. It is easy for therapists to become frustrated with parents' seeming lack of compliance and commitment, but in most cases the parents are well intentioned but have difficulty managing their time or priorities effectively. Generalization of skills and behaviors from the therapist's office to other settings has always been one of the most challenging aspects of intervention. Implementation problems are to be expected. Therapists who patiently work through the logistics with parents, fully recognizing the many demands on family time and energy, are likely to meet with eventual success.

Filial therapists stay alert for signs that parents' play session skills might be slipping. If therapists can maintain an accepting, nonjudgmental climate during therapy sessions, parents are more likely to give accurate appraisals of their use of the skills at home. When parents report negative reactions of children during play sessions, the therapist might want to examine possible declines in the use of skills as a contributing factor. The self-supervision questions that parents answer about each play session foster skill discussions, and occasional supervision of live play sessions can help therapists determine if erosion of skills is a problem. When it is, the therapist and parents discuss, model, or role-play the application of skills in the problematic situations.

Therapeutic Issues. Dynamic issues continue to surface via the play sessions even when the play sessions have been moved to the home. Discussion of play themes and meanings remains a major part of the therapy sessions. Parents continue to express concerns about their children and themselves as a consequence of play session events. The therapist handles them as before: showing acceptance of parents' feelings, reframing the problem when necessary, and moving the parents toward problem solving.

Home play sessions often see an increase in limit testing by some children. Children who have controlled their behavior in the therapist's playroom might decide to test the limits more vigorously at home. This can renew parents' fears that their children are becoming unruly as a result of the play sessions. This usually suggests that further work on the limit-setting skill is needed. Therapists can reassure parents that if they use the limit-setting skill effectively, the testing behavior is likely to fade.

Perhaps one of the most common concerns for parents during this period occurs when children play repetitively, with little or no variation in activities or themes from one session to the next. Parents frequently report that the sessions are boring, that they may be doing something incorrectly, or that they suspect that the play sessions no longer serve a purpose. Exactly the opposite may be true. Play that appears to be "stuck" often suggests that children are working through something significant. They might be trying to master a particular skill, integrate some new understanding of their world, or cope with a difficult problem. Sometimes, repetitive play indicates that parents might be showing understanding only at a superficial level and missing some of the key communications of the play. Therapists can check to see if parents' empathic responses are at the deepest level and help refine them if they are not.

Perhaps the best way for the therapist to determine if children are bored is to assess the degree of interest the child shows in the play session. If the child seems interested and involved in the play, then the therapist explains to parents that although the play seems boring from an adult perspective, it very likely has meaning for the child. Patience is encouraged. If the child has already dealt with most therapeutic issues and plays halfheartedly, as if going through the motions, then the therapist should evaluate whether it's time to use "special times," which will be described later (p. 69), in lieu of the play sessions.

If it has not arisen earlier, disagreement between parents on child-rearing issues often surfaces during the generalization phase of Filial Therapy. When attention shifts to parents' use of skills in everyday life, stylistic and philosophical differences emerge. Frequently, the resolution of those differences resides within the skills themselves. Differences often reflect preferences in the direction of permissiveness or stricter discipline. The filial and parenting skills emphasize a balance between nurturance and discipline. As the therapist shows parents how to adapt the skills to a broader range of situations, parents develop a better understanding of their selective use. The final chapter in L. F. Guerney's (1995) parenting skills book discusses ways parents can prioritize and balance the use of skills and is a good resource for this problem.

CASE STUDY

We used one therapy session to prepare for the transfer of play sessions to the Taylors' home. They decided to use their large kitchen for their play sessions, and they planned to keep the toys in their bedroom closet when not in use. Each parent would keep the remaining child busy while the others were having their play session, and they would let their answering machine take phone calls if the "nonplaying" parent was unable to answer the phone. The Taylors led busy lives, so finding times for the play sessions was difficult, but they eventually reached an agreement. They had found the process interesting so far, and each parent planned to hold a play session with each child per week.

For the first 2 weeks, the children's play was quite similar to their previous play. Jessi increased her limit testing during her first home session with Carol, but did not persist. Ed and Carol noticed some differences emerging during the third week at home.

Josh's play became more active but remained along the same themes. Jessi had one session where she invented a game she called "drop the baby" using the doll family. All members of the doll family took turns dropping the baby from various locations in the dollhouse, including the roof. After that, Jessi began playing with the water and baby bottles. She had several sessions with both parents in which she played a baby, talked baby talk, and had the parent do everything she wanted for nearly the entire session. She sucked her thumb, drank from the baby bottles, and asked Carol or Ed to hold her and sing songs. She also ordered them to perform a variety of tasks around the room. Eventually, she decided to become the parent and allowed Ed or Carol to be the baby. From that point, her play began to have more variety. She periodically played card games of her own design, and after the weeks of baby play, she occasionally set the game up so that whichever parent was playing with her would win, another change.

As might be expected, Carol and Ed were concerned about the "drop the baby game" when it occurred, and they tired of the "baby Jessi" play. They reported feeling bored during those sessions and asked me if there was anything they could do to "stimulate" her play. We fully discussed the potential meanings of these themes, and I suggested that although it may be tiresome for them to "do her bidding" each session, it was likely that she was working through some very important feelings about her "baby brother." They seemed to be using their skills well, and I encouraged their patience. They were quite pleased when her play became less self-centered and showed signs of nurturing others.

During the weeks that Jessi played the baby, her teacher told the parents that she had noticed some improvement in her behavior at school. She had been aware that Jessi was in therapy, and she called Carol to say that it seemed to be helping. Ed and Carol also reported that while she still teased Josh at home, she seemed to be more playful and less cruel. Jessi began playing "teacher" with Josh on occasion, and Carol and Ed believed that usually led to positive interactions between the children.

We began to work on the expanded use of parenting skills shortly after the Taylors began their home sessions. In this context, Carol told me she had used empathic listening one day when Jessi had been rejected by her friends at school. Carol said her usual response had been to question Jessi about what she had done to provoke it, and when she listened better, she was able to see the hurt that Jessi felt. Jessi had opened up to her more, and Carol could see some hope for their relationship. Ed and Carol worked through some of their tensions about limit setting at home using the three-step sequence whenever possible. They eventually agreed to a general set of limits and consequences, and they decided to consult together on other infractions. They also made an effort to use positive reinforcement more frequently with both children.

A combination of Filial play sessions and parenting skills had begun to result in an alleviation of the problems at home and more positive interactions among family members. The Taylors had conducted 16 home sessions over 8 weeks with each child when we began to discuss discharge from therapy.

THE CLOSING PHASE
OF FILIAL THERAPY

Filial therapists continue to meet with parents on a regular basis to discuss the home play sessions and to facilitate the generalization of the skills to daily life. As progress is made toward therapy goals, they begin to plan for the final phase of Filial Therapy.

HOW DISCHARGE IS DETERMINED

Filial Therapy is based upon an educational, competence model of intervention, and therapists guard against fostering unnecessary dependence in their client families. They attend to signs that indicate it is time to bring the therapy to a close. Several factors are considered.

First, it is usually evident much earlier in the therapy process if there is a poor fit between Filial Therapy and the family's problems, or if the family is unable or unwilling to make the commitment to conduct

Filial play sessions. An adjustment in therapeutic approach needs to be made as soon as lack of progress is noted. That adjustment might entail troubleshooting with the family to identify and correct the obstacles, or, if the family chooses not to follow through with Filial Therapy, the selection of another intervention such as therapist-conducted play therapy or behavior therapy, or referral to another therapist. There are times, although rare, when the therapist may need to discharge the family from therapy because their lack of cooperation prevents progress from being made. Care is taken to find solutions without blaming the family, but when all else fails, discharge is probably appropriate.

Second, the therapist can begin final discharge planning when the presenting problems are nearing resolution or are resolved. When behavioral goals have been established at the outset of therapy, it is easy to determine when they have been reached.

Third, another sign that Filial Therapy is in the closing phase comes from the children. A reduction in the children's interest in the play sessions coupled with a decrease in the intensity or thematic nature of the play might signal that the therapeutic value of the play sessions is nearing an end. Filial therapists need to rule out other reasons for children's lack of interest, such as poorly scheduled sessions that compete with favorite activities. If no such conditions exist and the children have already played through their significant problems, then discharge can be considered.

Fourth, when significant progress has been made and the therapist believes that the parents have developed a high degree of understanding of Filial Therapy and the application of parenting skills, then therapy can be phased out, allowing parents to continue play sessions on their own.

THE DISCHARGE PROCESS

Discharge planning begins with a discussion between the therapist and the parents about the final phase of therapy. The therapist and parents evaluate the progress that has been made and identify remaining problems. A joint decision is made to consider a phased-out discharge.

The therapist usually asks to observe a live play session, preferably with each parent. During this observation, the therapist notices each parent's skill and the quality of the play session, the interactions between the child and the parent, and the presence or absence of clinically significant behaviors or play themes. If the observed play sessions bear out earlier impressions that the problems are resolving well and that parents are ably conducting the play sessions, then the discharge process continues.

The therapist asks parents to complete any questionnaires, skill measures, or behavior rating scales administered during the assessment phase to provide additional evidence of progress. It is useful to share and discuss comparisons of the pre- and post-tests with the parents.

If discharge is indicated, the therapist prepares parents for the future use of play sessions without therapist supervision. Specifically, the therapist emphasizes the desirability of continuing play sessions until children grow tired of them. When children lose interest in the play sessions, parents are encouraged to hold "special times" with their children for at least one half-hour each week in lieu of the play sessions.

Special times are child centered in nature as well. Parents allow the children to choose from an acceptable range of activities and then remain as empathic and nondirective as possible, following the child's lead. Special times can include playing board games, going to the park, playing "catch" with a ball, sitting and talking about issues of importance to the children, going out to eat, or any other activity that allows uninterrupted interaction and full attention on the children. Special times are recommended on a one-to-one basis between parents and children similar to the play sessions, but they can also be extended to special family times in which the entire family participates in pleasant activities together.

Depending on the family's needs, the therapist arranges a phased-out meeting schedule with the parents. For example, if therapy meetings have been held biweekly to discuss home sessions, the therapist might suggest that they meet again in 4 to 6 weeks to ensure maintenance of gains. Follow-up telephone calls 3 and 6 months later can be planned to convey therapist support and interest. It is advisable to discuss this follow-up plan with parents to ensure that they do not perceive it as intrusive. It is vitally important that the therapist actually follow through with any plans made.

Finally, the therapist informs parents at their last meeting that they are welcome to return at any time with questions or concerns. Because parents have learned to use the various skills in many different situations, they are well prepared to handle recurring or new problems and are unlikely to need further assistance. The therapist wants to convey confidence in parents' ability to handle their own problems, but at the same time needs to keep the door open for future consultation if needed.

CASE STUDY

When it appeared that our therapy goals were being met and the Taylors were conducting play sessions and using parenting skills effectively, we discussed a phased-out termination plan. They brought the children in so I could observe Ed play with Josh and Carol play with Jessi. Both sessions were similar to the Taylors' descriptions of home sessions, and Jessi's play session demonstrated much more positive interaction between Jessi and her mother. Jessi invited Carol to take part in imaginary play scenarios that seemed playful and fun in tone.

I met with Carol and Ed 3 weeks later, and we had our last session a month after that. We agreed that nearly all goals had been met, and parent skill and child behavior measures confirmed that. I felt confident that the Taylors had the skills and knowledge needed to tackle the few remaining problems and others that might arise in the future.

They planned to continue with the play sessions at home, because everyone still enjoyed them. Carol told me during our last session that at first she had doubted the value of play in addressing their problems. Now she believed that the use of play sessions had helped her look beyond Jessi's outward behavior to the deeper issues and feelings that contributed to the problems. She also said it helped her to face some of her own feelings in a new, nonthreatening way. She indicated that the entire family seemed to be more playful as a result.

Ed indicated that he had been able to "loosen up" as a result of conducting the play sessions. He said that Carol and some coworkers had accused him of being too serious and reserved in the past, but he had recently been discovering more humor and fun in life. He found it "fascinating and refreshing" to see the world through his children's eyes, something he had not done before.

I spoke with the Taylors by telephone 4 and 8 months after their last session. They reported that their family relationships had continued to improve and they were doing well.

ALTERNATIVE FORMATS FOR FILIAL THERAPY

Filial Therapy was originally designed as a group model (Andronico et al., 1969; L. F. Guerney, 1991, 2003b; L. F. Guerney & Ryan, 2013) and can readily be adapted for use in a variety of formats. This section summarizes its use with individual families as covered throughout this guide, and then describes the use of Filial Therapy with groups of parents, with home-based intervention programs, in conjunction with other forms of therapy, as a prevention program, and as a very short-term intervention. The flexibility inherent in the Guerneys' Filial Therapy model have resulted in its use with full inclusion of the essential features in schools, community mental health centers, hospitals, and long-term disaster recovery programs. This section includes formats and applications of Filial Therapy that incorporate all of the essential features discussed early in this volume. A separate section provides information about interventions that are derived from Filial Therapy but that do not incorporate all of the essential features, and that can have somewhat different goals. Not covered here are some other interventions that bear resemblance to Filial Therapy in minor ways but cannot be considered as viable Filial Therapy interventions. It is important for practitioners to be able to evaluate interventions in terms of their allegiance to the Guerney Filial Therapy model as described in this volume and elsewhere (L. F. Guerney & Ryan, 2013), as that continues to be the gold standard in Filial Therapy. Consideration of the theories, principles, and essential features of Filial Therapy (pp. 3-16) is likely to provide a clearer picture of what is truly Filial Therapy and what is not. The greater the number of theories and essential features that are included, the more congruent the approach is with the original family therapy conceptualization and practice of Filial Therapy.

FORMAT FOR FILIAL THERAPY WITH INDIVIDUAL FAMILIES

Throughout this guide, Filial Therapy has been described as intended for use with individual families or single parents or caretakers. This format closely follows the original L. F. and B. G. Guerney model of Filial Therapy, and it includes all of the essential features of Filial Therapy. A sample outline of this individual family format follows, including the intake and therapy processes (VanFleet, 1999). This is based on 1-hour sessions.

Session #	Content of Session
1	Initial assessment, intake
2	Family play observation, discussion, recommendations
3	Play session demonstrations by therapist, discussion
4	Introduction of skills, parent practice of empathic listening
5-6	Mock play sessions with therapist playing the child and providing feedback
7-11	Supervised parent-child play sessions, discussions
12	Planning for transition to home play sessions
13	Discussion of first home play session
14-17	Discussion of home play sessions, skill generalization
18-20	Phased-out discharge process (sessions spread out over longer time period), discussion of home sessions, generalization, discharge

This outline can be altered in several ways, including more or fewer directly supervised play sessions and home session discussions. The typical number of sessions ranges from 15 to 25.

FILIAL THERAPY GROUPS: THE ORIGINAL GUERNEY MODEL

The original L. F. and B. G. Guerney group model of Filial Therapy continues to be an effective way of delivering this valuable intervention (see L. F. Guerney & Ryan, 2013 for full details). It should be noted that the long-term studies of Filial Therapy effectiveness were conducted using this model (see Filial Therapy Research section, pp. 18-21). This model includes all of the essential features of Filial Therapy.

Filial Therapy groups, composed of a maximum of six or eight parents, offer some advantages to the therapeutic process. Although they typically take longer, on average lasting 6 to 9 months (20 to 24 sessions), and sometimes are more cumbersome logistically, they provide an excellent means of increasing parental support and enhancing learning. The added dimensions of observational learning and peer interaction can be beneficial for all involved. Furthermore, costs to the families can be reduced when group formats are used. Smaller groups of three or four parents are conducted in the same manner, but typically take less time.

The playroom ideally is equipped with a one-way mirror and an observation booth from which the therapist and parents watch each other conducting their play sessions. Alternatively, using another room for the group to observe via a wireless camcorder/computer connection is satisfactory. Observation of the play sessions through an open door usually is not feasible with a group of parents as it is likely to distract the children and interfere with their play.

Groups can be formed following the child and family assessment process that is conducted with families separately. After the recommendation for Filial Therapy has been determined, the therapist suggests a group format for families who have mild to moderate problems. Families with severe or multiple problems are likely to require more individualized attention and may not be appropriate for a Filial Therapy group unless one is formed with their more significant needs in mind.

Groups can work well with families that are quite heterogeneous in terms both of background and presenting problems. The experience of parenting has so many common features that parents usually are able to relate well with each other even when their specific concerns are quite different. Because parents are learning new skills together, their prior educational or occupational backgrounds need not be of particular concern to the therapist when forming groups. Filial Therapy has an equalizing effect due to its skills-training nature. Although some parents are likely to master the skills more rapidly than others, they can serve as additional role models for the rest of the group. The therapist might want to weigh personality or style factors in the composition of groups, however.

Several modifications of the individual Filial Therapy process are needed for the group format. Additional time is needed during the first meetings for the group to become acquainted and to feel reasonably comfortable. The therapist discusses confidentiality with the group and obtains a commitment from each parent to maintain it.

The content and process of the training phase remains the same for Filial Therapy groups. Parents observe the therapist's play demonstrations with each family's children and then take turns practicing the skills. They watch each other's mock play sessions and listen to the therapist's feedback. After the feedback is given, the group is encouraged to enter the discussion and ask questions. Different issues are triggered by different play sessions, so the parents are often exposed to a wider range of situations during the group training process. The training phase usually lasts 2 months for Filial Therapy groups (L. F. Guerney & B. G. Guerney, 1987).

Filial Therapy groups seem to work best when meetings are held for 2 hours. When parents begin play sessions with their own children, the group usually observes two different parents conducting half-hour play sessions with their children, and in the final hour discusses what happened. In the same manner as described for individual families, the therapist provides feedback to the parents who conducted play sessions and then opens the discussion to the other parents. The therapist invites parents to comment or ask questions, carefully structuring interactions so that parents do not criticize each other's performance in the playroom. The therapist can prompt parents to note positive aspects of the play sessions, but provides all constructive criticism himself or herself.

Once home play sessions have begun, the therapist meets with the group on a weekly basis to process everyone's home sessions, to teach the parenting skills, and to help parents apply their skills to a variety of problematic situations. Again, the therapist structures the discussion to avoid advice-giving by other parents and focuses instead on children's play themes and applications of the skills.

A short break during the 2-hour group meeting is recommended. This helps maintain group interest and provides an opportunity for informal interaction and support among the parents. The provision of child care during Filial Therapy sessions, especially when two or more children must be present for supervised live play sessions, can add significantly to parents' ability to attend regularly. L.F. Guerney and Ryan (2013) have written a comprehensive manual that covers virtually every imaginable detail about group Filial Therapy.

FILIAL THERAPY AS A HOME-BASED INTERVENTION

Funding exists for some agencies to provide services to families within the home setting under special circumstances. This may be necessary in rural areas or for multiproblem families needing more intensive intervention. Filial Therapy can easily be adapted to in-home services.

In this case, filial therapists create traveling play kits consisting of the same toys used in a child-centered playroom. They work with the families to designate a play area, set up the toys, and conduct Filial Therapy much as they would in an office setting. Therapists choose an unobtrusive location from which to watch the play sessions, often in a corner of the room. In a mobile home, for example, a therapist can sit in the living room and observe a play session being held in the kitchen area.

When the play session is over, the therapist quickly collects the Filial Therapy toys to eliminate the temptation for children to continue playing with them, and then meets with the parents to discuss the session.

One of the biggest difficulties in home-based interventions can be the interruptions or disorganization in the family's lifestyle. The home-based Filial therapist can discuss ways for the parents to structure the environment and can model how to do this. For example, the therapist might need to ask the parents politely to turn off the television while they are talking and holding play sessions. In general, however, few modifications to Filial Therapy are necessary for home-based programs, perhaps because it has been designed for use at home.

USE OF FILIAL THERAPY WITH OTHER INTERVENTIONS

Filial Therapy can work well in conjunction with other interventions. For example, crisis intervention, behavior therapy, or psychiatric consultation may be required when children or families with serious problems need immediate relief. Parents may need marital therapy when problems between them extend beyond parenting issues. Individual therapy may be indicated for parents experiencing significant depression. Ginsberg (1997, 2003) has provided a framework for blending different interventions or using them sequentially with Filial Therapy.

Even when families have numerous problems, therapists must avoid overwhelming them with therapy. Prioritizing the family's needs can help the therapist direct interventions to core problems. Family input is valuable in setting priorities, but therapists' clinical knowledge and judgment are important as well.

When other interventions are used simultaneously with Filial Therapy, therapists need to guard against "contamination" of the child-centered, competence-based nature of Filial Therapy. It can be confusing for children when the same playroom is used for both child-centered and directive types of play therapy. In such cases, it is better to conduct the two interventions in different rooms so the child has a clear, concrete understanding of the different structure, roles, and "rules" of the therapies. Such a change in environment is usually sufficient, but if children seem confused in spite of the use of different rooms, separate therapists for the different interventions might be desirable. At other times when there is just a single room available, a simple explanation by the therapist can distinguish the Filial Therapy sessions from other directive play therapy interventions: "Merilee, today we'll start where you'll have your special play time with your father. After that, I have another activity I would like us to try."

In some cases, the use of Filial Therapy is preceded by child-centered play therapy, perhaps due to the severity of the child problems, parental inability to participate from the beginning, or other reasons. In these cases, the therapist structures a transition over to the parent-led sessions while phasing out his or her own nondirective play sessions. This is done to further empower the parents and to avoid tensions that can arise when the therapist is providing a duplicate of what the parents are now offering. To transition, the parents are invited, with the child's knowledge, to observe one or two of the therapist-conducted sessions. After the parents are trained and ready to start the actual sessions, therapist-led and parent-led play sessions can be alternated through two or three cycles, after which the parents assume responsibility for all of the nondirective play sessions.

In general, Filial Therapy can be used in conjunction with other therapies, but the therapist needs to consider carefully the implications of each therapy for the other. Such forethought can prevent the family from perceiving "mixed messages" from the therapeutic process.

FILIAL THERAPY AS A PREVENTION PROGRAM

Because Filial Therapy is designed to strengthen family relation-ships using the natural modality of play, it can readily be used as an educational prevention program. Children and families with no significant problems can benefit from Filial Therapy by increasing their ability to understand and relate to each other, by having fun together, and by appreciating more fully the complexities of child and family development. When parents can create and maintain a family atmosphere of open communication, commitment to each other, and fun, they might be able to offset potential problems.

When using Filial Therapy as a prevention program, therapists follow the same sequence of training, supervised play sessions, and home sessions that they use when conducting therapy with troubled children and families. Play themes emerge in the play of well-adjusted children, too, and the therapist discusses them with the parents in terms of what issues or concerns are relevant to the child at that time. Many times the themes reflect developmental features such as mastery of skills, understanding of family roles, concern about peer relationships, and self-esteem. Parents usually enjoy the new understanding of their children's emotional and social development that they gain through their play.

Filial Therapy usually takes less time with families who engage in it for relationship-enhancement purposes. The play themes take less time to work through, and parents do not have as many personal issues to resolve. Coufal and Brock (1983) and Landreth and Bratton (2006) have each developed a 10-week parent education program using play sessions based on Filial Therapy that are also well-suited for prevention programs.

VERY BRIEF FORMATS FOR FILIAL THERAPY

Filial Therapy as originally conceived, researched, and reported in this guide is a relatively short-term intervention. Nevertheless, constraints on time and funding sometimes necessitate interventions that are fewer than 10 to 12 weeks in duration. Very brief individual and group formats that preserve the essential elements of Filial Therapy have been developed. Ginsberg (1997) and VanFleet (2000, 2003b) have described 10-week formats for Filial Therapy with individual families. *The Casebook of Filial Therapy* contains detailed descriptions of format adaptations of Filial Therapy as well (VanFleet & L. F. Guerney, 2003).

FILIAL THERAPY GROUP FORMAT
FOR FOSTER AND ADOPTIVE FAMILIES

VanFleet, Sniscak, and Faa-Thompson (2013) use a 14- to 18-week group Filial Therapy format with foster and adoptive families, focusing on children with serious trauma and attachment problems. This program retains all the essential features of Filial Therapy and adds components that specifically address the very challenging issues that often arise in these families. This format can be adapted for other families facing serious difficulties as well.

This group approach typically has 3-hour sessions and uses two leaders to provide sufficient supervision and support to parents as they practice skills and hold play sessions. The group meets together for didactic presentations and discussions, and divides into two smaller groups for the hands-on portions. It provides additional information about the links between trauma and attachment and children's feelings and behaviors, providing a template for understanding the often-extreme behaviors parents face. Additional mock play sessions often are added to ensure parents' preparation for intense play themes and strong challenges to the limits.

This approach can be used as part of a novel foster-to-adopt transition model that encourages the collaborative use of Filial Therapy with foster parents during placement and adoptive parents early in the adoption process (VanFleet, 2006c).

OTHER FILIAL THERAPY-DERIVED
OR -INSPIRED PROGRAMS AND ADAPTATIONS

Filial Therapy as described in this book is flexible and can be used for many different problems and in a wide range of settings and circumstances. To be assured of the most effective and long-lasting family systems results, it is important to maintain as many of the essential features of Filial Therapy as possible (VanFleet, 2011c). Even so, today's economic climate coupled with changing philosophies of mental health service delivery result in situations where some of the essential features sometimes must be omitted if Filial Therapy is to be offered at all. There are times when creativity is needed, and funding or time constraints mean that "something has to give." The key when altering such a powerful family intervention as Filial Therapy is to be thoughtful when doing so and to consider what is gained and what is lost when making fundamental alterations to the method (VanFleet, 2011c). This section provides information and resources about several such programs that are likely to be useful to some readers.

At present, there are several other programs and formats that have been developed and studied through the years. For the programs described below, one or more of the essential features of Filial Therapy have been omitted, but the goals of these programs vary to some extent from the full family therapy goals of the original Guerney model, so those features may be less relevant to those purposes. In each case, the program was derived from or inspired by Filial Therapy, and they are offered here as beneficial alternatives that can be very useful for children and families. References to still other adaptations of Filial Therapy are also included in the section called Applications of Filial Therapy to Specialized Populations (pp. 81-87)

CHILD-PARENT RELATIONSHIP THERAPY (CPRT)

Landreth and Bratton (2006) have established a strong foundation for their 10-week group program based on Filial Therapy. This format provides a viable alternative with a parent education program flavor. In order to reduce the number of sessions, they have created an alternate route for training parents, reduced the amount of supervision of parents' filial play sessions, and limited the play sessions to one parent and one child rather than all of the children. Their manualized approach has spawned considerable positive research and offers strong advantages over other parent education models. Their emphasis on the skills and importance of empathy and acceptance through the use of play is invaluable in the development of effective child-rearing skills for parents. Considerable research on this method with many different presenting issues has shown significant parent gains (see some references in the Research section, pp. 18-21). *The Casebook of Filial Therapy* (VanFleet & L. F. Guerney, 2003) contains numerous chapters highlighting the CPRT approach as well. Practitioners of the CPRT method continue to add steadily to the growing literature on Filial Therapy effectiveness.

PERNET-CAPLIN FILIAL THERAPY
GROUP FORMAT FOR DISADVANTAGED FAMILIES

Pernet and Caplin (in progress) developed their 12-week group Filial Therapy program for disadvantaged families at the Children's Crisis Treatment Center in Philadelphia, Pennsylvania, where it has been used for many years. Their format has been used with victims of Hurricane Katrina in New Orleans as well. Two leaders meet with the entire group for didactic portions of Filial Therapy and then provide direct supervision in smaller groups. To reduce the number of sessions overall while still providing considerable live observation and feedback to parents during their play sessions, Pernet and Caplin have decreased the play sessions from the usual 30 minutes to 10 minutes each (until the home session phase when they increase to 30 minutes each). This adjustment to the timing keeps the play sessions manageable for families with multiple needs while providing direct parent skill development and support, and more informed discussion of the children's developing play themes.

WRIGHT-WALKER GROUP FILIAL
THERAPY FOR HEAD START FAMILIES

Described in detail in the *Casebook of Filial Therapy* (Wright & Walker, 2003), this format uses two coleaders for groups of approximately 10 parents. Because the families involved in Head Start often have many needs, this program has provided transportation, meals, and toy-making materials and opportunities to assist parents and encourage attendance. At the request of parents, the program was expanded to a 13-week format, with the last session spaced a bit further from the others to assist with the skill generalization process. One empowering adjustment has been to enlist the assistance of one or two parents from prior Filial Therapy groups to demonstrate the play sessions for the new group. The two group leaders meet with the entire group for information-giving and discussion, and then break into two smaller groups, each with a single leader, for actual skill practice and observation of actual parent-child play sessions. Individual feedback is provided to each parent within the smaller groups. At the final session, the group watches a pre- and post-video of each parent's play sessions, and parent improvements are celebrated.

APPLICATIONS OF FILIAL THERAPY
TO SPECIALIZED POPULATIONS

Filial Therapy has been used widely to help meet the needs of specialized populations. The *Casebook of Filial Therapy* (VanFleet & L.F. Guerney, 2003) describes many adaptations to diverse populations, settings, and cultures in detail. Some of these applications are briefly described below.

CHILDREN OF DIVORCE

The social and emotional needs of children of divorce have been well documented (Wallerstein & Blakeslee, 1989; Wallerstein & Kelly, 1980). Once parents have dealt with their own feelings sufficiently to be able to concentrate on their children's needs, Filial Therapy can offer a means of resolving the children's feelings and rebuilding the relationship between the children and the parents. Filial Therapy can be conducted with one or both of the parents, depending on their willingness to cooperate with each other. Because children of divorce can have strong fantasies about their parents reuniting, it is often advisable to conduct Filial Therapy with each side of the family separately. If amicably divorced parents were to attend therapy together, it might give children the mistaken impression that the play sessions would help bring their parents back together. Bratton and Crane (2003) have described a brief group intervention with single parents.

CHILDREN WITH SCHOOL PROBLEMS

School problems can be the result of social, emotional, behavioral, or family difficulties. Persistent academic problems can lead to an erosion of children's self-esteem and confidence. Filial Therapy can help children cope with the emotional aspects of these problems and help parents deal with their children's feelings and behavior more effectively. L. F. Guerney (1983b) has described the use of Filial Therapy with learning disabled children. One innovative program combining Filial Therapy and Adlerian principles has involved primary grade teachers in special play sessions with some of the at-risk students in their classes (White, Draper, & Flynt, 2003). Another has incorporated Filial Therapy into a program for parents earning GEDs (Reynolds, 2003). Carmen Baldus and Mark King have created a Filial Therapy-inspired program for elementary teachers in Michigan, including generalization of the skills for classroom and group use (personal communication). It is hoped that materials about their program will be available in the future.

DEPRESSED CHILDREN

Sometimes when depressed children are reluctant or unable to talk about their problems, they will express them through their play. Filial Therapy can help parents become more sensitive to their children's needs, and it can help identify and correct some of the family problems that might be contributing to the depression.

ADOPTIVE AND FOSTER CHILDREN

Adoptive and foster children often have many areas of need. Their backgrounds may have made them feel vulnerable and distrustful of adults. Filial Therapy can provide a method for developing attachments to their adoptive or foster parents. It can also give the children an opportunity to work through their feelings in a supportive, nonjudgmental environment. Filial Therapy has the potential to stabilize placements for these children, as well as give them an experience or model of healthy relationships. Ginsberg (1989) and VanFleet (1994, 2003a) have written about the use of Filial Therapy with adoptive families. Others have described its application to kinship care (Malon, 2003), foster care (Sweeney, 2003), and family reunification (Lilly, 2003). A novel foster-to-adopt transition model featuring Filial Therapy with both foster and adoptive families has been described by VanFleet (2006c), and a 14- to 18-week group program for foster and adoptive families is detailed by VanFleet, Sniscak, and Faa-Thompson (2013).

CHILDREN WITH CHRONIC ILLNESSES

Chronic illnesses often place restrictions on children's and families' lives and remove their sense of control. Filial Therapy provides children with an experience of control in the play sessions, and it gives parents a way to improve the quality of family life at a time when they might be feeling quite helpless (VanFleet, 1992, 2000, 2003b). It also provides support for siblings of ill children who might get reduced parental attention due to the illness and treatment demands on the family. Filial Therapy can be adapted for use with hospitalized children as well as with families where one of the parents is ill.

ANXIOUS AND
PERFECTIONISTIC CHILDREN

Filial Therapy can also be applied to children with various types of anxiety problems. Children with strong perfectionistic tendencies seem to experience anxiety, fear of failure, and inhibited risk taking. The use of play in a Filial Therapy context can help these children deal with their fears and concerns while increasing their parents' sensitivity to factors that might be causing the anxiety problems (VanFleet, 1997). Filial Therapy has helped anxious parents become more relaxed and playful as well.

CHILDREN WITH
ELIMINATION PROBLEMS

Enuresis and encopresis have emotional roots in many cases. If biological causes have been ruled out, Filial Therapy can offer children an opportunity to explore and express their feelings through play. It can also help parents better understand their children's conflicts, respond to them in a supportive manner, and apply parenting skills in a manner more likely to lead to positive results. Filial Therapy can easily be used in conjunction with other behavioral and medical interventions.

CHILDREN OF ADDICTED
OR RECOVERING PARENTS

Living with a parent who has an addiction problem usually is confusing at best. Family dynamics are often askew, leaving children in a vulnerable position. Filial Therapy can be conducted with the nonaddicted parent or with parents in recovery. Play therapy or other interventions may be desirable to help children deal with their issues initially, but Filial Therapy can be used to reestablish damaged relationships within the family. Filial Therapy is compatible with 12-step recovery programs.

CHILDREN WITH ATTENTION
DEFICIT PROBLEMS

Filial Therapy can be used or adapted for children with attention-deficit/hyperactivity disorder, primarily to address self-esteem and relationship problems that arise. Often families coping with ADHD become frustrated with the child's behavior, and a negatively focused parent-child relationship ensues. Although other interventions can help with the specific attentional problems, Filial Therapy can help provide a supportive environment for the child and a less frustrating one for the parents (Sniscak, 2003). Most children with ADHD respond well to Filial Therapy with few modifications, but if the child is easily distracted, using fewer toys in a smaller space can help.

ABUSED AND NEGLECTED CHILDREN

Children who have been abused usually experience problems with their self-concepts, their emotional development, and their interpersonal relationships. When one of the parents has been the perpetrator of abuse, it is advisable to provide the parties involved with other types of therapy prior to Filial Therapy. In this case, Filial Therapy would not be used to address clinical issues stemming from the abuse but to help with family reintegration if that is the goal set by child protective service authorities. Various interventions, including play therapy, that help the children express and work through their feelings are needed first. Similarly, the parents initially require individual and marital therapy to address their problems. Filial Therapy can be useful after these initial interventions have benefited the children and parents. It can be used to help parents learn how to play and interact positively with their children and to teach parents how to set and enforce limits effectively without abusing their children. In many ways, Filial Therapy can be used to prevent future abuse by providing the family members with new ways of relating to each other. Lilly (2003) has described the use of Filial Therapy for family reunification. If children are removed from the home, Filial Therapy has been used extensively with foster parents, as noted earlier.

CHILDREN WITH ATTACHMENT DISRUPTIONS AND DISORDERS

Children with attachment problems pose special challenges to their parents, caregivers, case managers, and therapists. Attachment problems arise from many different circumstances, including separations from parents, traumatic events, anxious parenting styles, temperamental and biomedical factors, lack of physical or emotional safety, inconsistency in the child's environment, abusive caretakers, frequent changes in living conditions, or even decisions made by the child protective system

(Bernstein, 2001; James, 1994; VanFleet & Sniscak, 2003a). Healthy attachments provide a protective shield around family members that help them cope with difficult life circumstances (Figley, 1989; Sroufe, 1983; Sroufe & Rutter, 1984). The manner in which healthy attachments occur (Ainsworth, 1982; Belsky & Nezworski, 1988; Bowlby, 1982; Brazelton & Cramer, 1990) can serve as a guide to interventions designed to alleviate attachment problems in children. Ryan has suggested that nondirective play therapy recreates many of the interactions that lead to healthy attachment in infancy (Ryan, 2007; Ryan & Wilson, 1995). Filial Therapy has been used successfully to address complex attachment problems, including reactive attachment disorder, either as a sole treatment or as the core intervention in a multimodal treatment approach (Topham, VanFleet, & Sniscak, 2013; VanFleet, 2006c; VanFleet & Sniscak, 2003a; VanFleet, Sniscak, & Faa-Thompson, 2013).

CHILDREN EXPOSED TO DOMESTIC VIOLENCE

When children see one of their parents being treated violently or abusively, they typically have strong reactions. They can feel helpless, frightened, and guilty for not being able to protect their parent. The impact of family violence can be as devastating as if the abuse were directed at the children. Sometimes parents who have been subjected to domestic violence worry that their children will become perpetrators as well, and some parents even become rejecting of children who remind them of the perpetrator. There are many needs in these families, but Filial Therapy can help them form healthier bonds as they begin a healing process together. Filial Therapy has been adapted for use in domestic violence shelters and community programs (Barabash, 2003; Ramos, 2003).

CHILDREN WITH OPPOSITIONAL DEFIANT DISORDER

Oppositional behavior in children is often related to a breakdown in the parent-child hierarchy, closely related to parenting issues. It can also have its roots in anxiety, frustration, and insecurity for the child. Filial Therapy provides the means by which children can more appropriately express and work through their anxieties and by which parents can reassert their authority through the use of both empathy and firm boundaries. Sywulak (2003) has described the use of Filial Therapy with this population.

CHILDREN WITH AUTISM
SPECTRUM DISORDERS

Filial Therapy offers several potential benefits to families of children with Autism Spectrum Disorders (ASD) (VanFleet, 2012b). The child-centered play sessions provide a unique form of communication and expression for children. Even though their play differs from that of typically developing children, children with ASD do play, and the child-centered play sessions provide them with safety and choices without pressure. There is no need for them to communicate verbally, as they can readily communicate nonverbally through play. Siblings can also benefit from the play sessions, especially if their own lives have been more isolated or consumed with matters pertaining to their brother or sister with ASD. Perhaps the biggest value of Filial Therapy for these families is through its empowerment of the parents, giving them new tools with which to understand and communicate with their children. Parents of children with ASD who have participated in Filial Therapy have reported a large sense of relief as they learn that the communication channels have opened in this unique,way

MILITARY FAMILIES

Military families face unique stresses with frequent moves and separations during deployments. Deployments and reunions necessitate substantial role changes. During times of war or heightened military alert, families encounter greater worry about their deployed relatives, especially when communications are prohibited or erratic. Injuries and sometimes death are difficult for everyone to think about or cope with. Children are vulnerable under these conditions and may display their anxieties through internalizing, externalizing, and trauma reactions. Filial Therapy has been used with military families when they are together and when they are separated by deployments. It helps strengthen family relationships, gives children an outlet for their concerns, provides parents with the tools needed to meet their children's emotional needs more fully, and offers parents substantial support during difficult times. Filial Therapy can also help families develop or maintain the flexibility needed for constantly changing conditions.

CHILDREN OF
FIRST RESPONDERS

Children whose parents are first responders (i.e., law enforcement officers, fire fighters, and other rescue personnel) sometimes experience anxieties due to the unique nature of their parent's work. Children might worry each time their parent is called out, often in the middle of the night, to the scene of sometimes dangerous situations. They might worry every day that their first responder parent leaves for work, wondering if that parent will be safe. Parents whose work places them in contact with intense human circumstances or the "darker side" of life sometimes have difficulty shifting from their work world to their home life. They might need to "shut down" emotionally at times in order to function in their first responder roles. Filial Therapy has been used to help families of first responders to remain emotionally connected with each other, to alleviate children's fears about their parent's work and safety, and to provide an emotionally safe environment in which family members can enjoy each other.

FAMILIES EXPERIENCING TRAUMATIC EVENTS

Filial Therapy can help families who have experienced a wide range of traumatic events, such as car accidents, house fires, natural disasters, violence, war, terrorism, school threats or shootings, racism or genocide, and industrial disasters. Research suggests that family cohesiveness can ameliorate the impact of trauma on children (Figley, 1989; Garbarino et al.,1992; Garbarino, Kostelny, & Dubrow, 1991). There are nearly always family effects of trauma, even when the traumatic event happens to just one family member (Figley, 1989). Filial Therapy helps children with their reactions, supports parents during immensely difficult times, and provides family members with new ways of interacting as they face the aftermath of trauma and try to move forward. Filial Therapy has been used successfully with families experiencing most types of natural disasters, with families affected directly and indirectly by September 11, 2001, and similar violent acts, with families living in war zones, and with families experiencing a wide range of traumatic loss, such as accidental deaths or murder (Mochi & VanFleet, 2009; VanFleet & Mochi, in press; VanFleet & Sniscak, 2003b).

MULTICULTURAL
APPLICABILITY OF FILIAL THERAPY

Filial Therapy has been used with families representing a wide range of ethnic and cultural backgrounds throughout the world. Although adjustments must be made to accommodate cultural beliefs and practices, it seems well-suited for multicultural use (e.g., see VanFleet & L. F. Guerney, 2003). The values of Filial Therapy are consistent with many cultures, and most cultures value strong family systems. Filial Therapy books, manuals, DVDs, and other materials developed by the author of this volume have been used in over 75 countries, and some materials have been translated into several languages. Several factors may account for the multicultural applicability of Filial Therapy.

First, children's play is universal. If given the opportunity, children play, and they play within the cultural environment in which they live. The nondirective play therapy methods used in Filial Therapy permit children to play out their concerns within their own cultural context.

Second, when therapists work with children who are culturally different from them, there is a heightened risk that they will misinterpret the child's play, even when they try to be culturally sensitive. In Filial Therapy, the parents play a large role in understanding their children's play themes, lessening the likelihood that a cultural misinterpretation will take place. The Filial Therapy emphasis on a contextual understanding of play themes and reliance on parents' knowledge of their own children creates a unique environment for collaboration.

Third, in Filial Therapy, respect for the family is paramount. Filial therapists try to develop open, empathic, and genuine relationships with the parents, and they encourage parents to speak freely, even if they disagree with the therapist. Furthermore, if parents do disagree with the therapist, the therapist empathically listens to them, and this in turn fosters greater trust and honest communication. When working with culturally different clients, Filial therapists invite the parents to educate them about cultural practices, beliefs, symbols, interpretations, and so on. This interaction style applies to all parents in Filial Therapy, but it contributes to greater ethnic understanding. This relationship-based form of cultural sensitivity can result in a true partnership between parent and therapist, with a common goal of helping the child (VanFleet, 2004).

DEVELOPING COMPETENCE
IN FILIAL THERAPY

Filial Therapy may sound like a simple intervention, but it is not. Family therapy is never simple, and Filial Therapy requires a sophisticated knowledge of family therapy, play therapy, behavior therapy, cognitive therapy, client-centered therapy, and a working knowledge of child development, attachment theory, and family development. It also requires a set of finely tuned interpersonal skills and especially, empathy. All of this is then integrated in the unique manner of working called Filial Therapy.

Filial Therapy requires more than reading a book or watching a DVD to master. These materials provide an excellent introduction, but to practice Filial Therapy ethically and effectively, one must be trained thoroughly in it and receive feedback when implementing it with client families. This is true for experienced practitioners, too, because Filial Therapy is quite different from other forms of intervention, and there are subtleties of practice that are difficult to convey in writing. Even so, many clinicians who have achieved proficiency in Filial Therapy have considered the route well worth it. Seeing the gains made by parents and children and the warmth and closeness shared by them is very rewarding.

To do Filial Therapy well, one must first be able to conduct child-centered play therapy competently. After that, it is appropriate to attend a class or intensive workshop that teaches the skills of Filial Therapy in depth. The best trainings are those in which participants have the opportunity to practice the skills and methods of every major stage of Filial Therapy. Training programs that are taught using the same principles and methods to teach professionals as are used to teach parents in Filial Therapy are ideal. Advanced training programs help practitioners hone their skills after they have worked with several families under supervision.

A set of credentials in Filial Therapy is offered by the Family Enhancement & Play Therapy Center. The credentials are based on demonstrated competence and include Certified Filial Therapist, Certified Filial Therapy Supervisor, and Certified Filial Therapy Instructor.

More information about training programs in the United States and abroad in child-centered play therapy, Filial Therapy, and other topics can be obtained from the contact information below.

Risë VanFleet, Ph.D., RPT-S, CDBC
Family Enhancement & Play Therapy Center, Inc.
PO Box 613, Boiling Springs, PA 17007 USA
Phone: 717-249-4707
Website: www.risevanfleet.com
Emails: rise@risevanfleet.com or risevanfleet@aol.com

SUMMARY

Filial Therapy is an intervention with wide applicability for children with social, emotional, and behavioral problems stemming from a variety of sources. It uses a psychoeducational intervention model which is based on client-centered, dynamic, behavioral, cognitive, interpersonal, developmental, and family systems principles.

In Filial Therapy, practitioners teach, supervise, and empower parents in the conduct of child-centered play sessions with their children. This approach addresses clinical issues while strengthening the relationships between children and parents. Filial Therapy is useful for families experiencing significant problems as well as for families who simply want to improve their relationships. It is a flexible approach that therapists can modify to meet the particular needs of the children and families whom they serve. Filial Therapy has the added advantage of being an enjoyable experience for the children, their parents, and the therapist.

Fifty years of research and clinical experience have consistently shown the value and effectiveness of Filial Therapy. The robustness of the approach has led to rapidly increasing international interest in Filial Therapy. Active dissemination, training, and research programs are helping professionals use Filial Therapy to prevent or solve child problems, increase parents' competence and confidence, and strengthen families throughout the world.

REFERENCES

Ainsworth, M. D. S. (1982). Attachment: Retrospect and prospect. In C. M. Parkes & J. Stevenson-Hinde (Eds.), *The Place of Attachment in Human Behavior*. New York: Basic Books.

Andronico, M. P., Fidler, J., Guerney, B. G., Jr., & Guerney, L. F. (1967). The combination of didactic and dynamic elements in filial therapy. *International Journal of Group Psychotherapy, 17,* 10-17.

Andronico, M. P., Fidler, J., Guerney, B. G., Jr., & Guerney, L. F. (1969). The combination of didactic and dynamic elements in filial therapy. In B. G. Guerney, Jr. (Ed.), *Psychotherapeutic Agents: New Roles for Nonprofessionals, Parents, and Teachers* (pp. 371-377). New York: Holt, Rinehart & Winston.

Andronico, M. P., & Guerney, B. G., Jr. (1969). A psychotherapeutic aide in a Head Start program. *Children, 16*(1), 14-22.

Axline, V. M. (1947). *Play Therapy.* Cambridge, MA: Houghton-Mifflin.

Axline, V. M. (1969). *Play Therapy* (rev. ed.). New York: Ballantine Books.

Barabash, K. J. (2003). *Developmental Filial Therapy: Process-Outcome Research on Strengthening Parent-Child Relationships through Play in a Setting for Victims of Domestic Violence.* Unpublished doctoral dissertation, University of Victoria, Victoria, British Columbia.

Belsky, J., & Nezworski, T. (Eds.). (1988). *Clinical Implications of Attachment.* Hillsdale, NJ: Lawrence Erlbaum Associates.

Bernstein, N. (2001). *The Lost Children of Wilder: The Epic Struggle to Change Foster Care.* New York: Pantheon Books.

Bifulco, A., & Thomas, G. (2012). *Understanding Adult Attachment in Family Relationships: Research, Assessment and Intervention.* London, England: Routledge.

Bowlby, J. (1982). *Attachment* (2nd ed.). New York: Basic Books.

Bratton, S. C., & Crane, J. M. (2003). Filial/family play therapy with single parents. In R. VanFleet & L. F. Guerney (Eds.), *Casebook of Filial Therapy* (pp. 139-162). Boiling Springs, PA: Play Therapy Press.

Bratton, S. C., & Landreth, G. (1995). Filial therapy with single parents: Effects on parental acceptance, empathy, and stress. *International Journal of Play Therapy, 4*(1), 61-80.

Bratton, S. C., Ray, D., Rhine, T., & Jones, L. (2005). The efficacy of play therapy with children: A meta-analytic review of treatment outcomes. *Professional Psychology: Research and Practice, 36*(4), 376-390.

Brazelton, T. B., & Cramer, B. G. (1990). *The Earliest Relationship: Parents, Infants, and the Drama of Early Attachment.* Cambridge, MA: Perseus Books.

Bronfenbrenner, U. (1979). *The Ecology of Human Development.* Cambridge, MA: Harvard University Press.

Cavedo, C., & Guerney, B.G. (1999). Relationship Enhancement (RE) enrichment/problem-prevention programs: Therapy-derived, powerful, versatile. In R. Berger & M.T. Hannah (Eds.), *Handbook of Preventive Approaches in Couples Therapy* (pp. 73-105). New York: Brunner/Mazel.

Chau, I., & Landreth, G. (1997). Filial therapy with Chinese parents: Effects on parental empathic interactions, parental acceptance of child and parental stress. *International Journal of Play Therapy, 6*(2), 75-92.

Costas, M., & Landreth, G. (1999). Filial therapy with non-offending parents of children who have been sexually abused. *International Journal of Play Therapy, 8*(1), 43-66.

Coufal, J. D., & Brock, G. W. (1983). *Parent-Child Relationship Enhancement: A 10-Week Education Program.* Menomonie, WI: Coufal & Brock.

Figley, C. R. (1989). *Helping Traumatized Families.* San Francisco, CA: Jossey-Bass.

Garbarino, J., Dubrow, N., Kostelny, K., & Pardo, C. (1992). *Children in Danger: Coping With the Consequences of Community Violence.* San Francisco, CA: Jossey-Bass.

Garbarino, J., Kostelny, K., & Dubrow, N. (1991). What children can tell us about living in danger. *American Psychologist, 46*(4), 376-383.

Ginsberg, B. G. (1989). Training parents as therapeutic agents with foster/adoptive children using the filial approach. In C. E. Schaefer & J. M. Briesmeister (Eds.), *Handbook of Parent Training* (pp. 442-478). New York: John Wiley & Sons.

Ginsberg, B. G. (1997). *Relationship Enhancement Family Therapy.* New York: John Wiley & Sons.

Ginsberg, B. G. (2003). An integrated holistic model of child-centered family therapy. In R. VanFleet & L. F. Guerney (Eds.), *Casebook of Filial Therapy* (pp. 21-47). Boiling Springs, PA: Play Therapy Press.

Gitlin-Weiner, K., Sandgrund, A., & Schaefer, C.E. (2000). *Play Diagnosis and Assessment.* Hoboken, NJ: John Wiley & Sons.

Glazer-Waldman, H. R. (1991). *Filial Therapy: CPR Training for Families With Chronically Ill Children.* Unpublished master's thesis, University of North Texas, Denton.

Glover, G., & Landreth, G. (2000). Filial therapy with Native Americans. *International Journal of Play Therapy, 9*(1), 57-80.

Grskovic, J. A., & Goetze, H. (2008). Short-term filial therapy with German mothers: Findings from a controlled study. *International Journal of Play Therapy, 17*(1), 39-51.

Guerney, B. G., Jr. (1964). Filial therapy: Description and rationale. *Journal of Consulting Psychology, 28,* 303-310.

Guerney, B. G., Jr., & Stover, L. (1971). *Filial Therapy: Final Report on MH 1826401.* Unpublished manuscript, The Pennsylvania State University, University Park, PA.

Guerney, L. F. (1975). *Follow-Up Study on Filial Therapy.* Paper presented at the annual convention of the Eastern Psychological Association, New York.

Guerney, L. F. (1976a). Filial therapy program. In D. H. Olson (Ed.), *Treating Relationships* (pp. 67-91). Lake Mills, IA: Graphic Publishing.

Guerney, L. F. (1976b). Training manual for parents: Instruction in filial therapy. In C. E. Schaefer (Ed.), *Therapeutic Use of Child's Play* (pp. 216-227). New York: Jason Aronson.

Guerney, L. F. (1983a). Introduction to filial therapy: Training parents as therapists. In P. A. Keller & L. G. Ritt (Eds.), *Innovations in*

Clinical Practice: A Source Book (Vol. 2, pp. 26-39). Sarasota, FL: Professional Resource Exchange.

Guerney, L. F. (1983b). Play therapy with learning disabled children. In C. E. Schaefer & K. J. O'Connor (Eds.), *Handbook of Play Therapy* (pp. 419-435). New York: John Wiley & Sons.

Guerney, L. F. (1987). *A Clinician's and Group Leader's Manual for Parenting: A Skills Training Program.* North Bethesda, MD: IDEALS.

Guerney, L. F. (1991). Parents as partners in treating behavior problems in early childhood settings. *Topics in Early Childhood Special Education, 11*(2), 74-90.

Guerney, L. F. (1995). *Parenting: A Skills Training Manual* (5th ed.). North Bethesda, MD: IDEALS.

Guerney, L. F. (1997). Filial therapy. In K. O'Connor & L. Braverman (Eds.), *Play Therapy: Theory and Practice* (pp. 131-159). New York: John Wiley & Sons.

Guerney, L. F. (2000). Filial therapy into the 21st century. *International Journal of Play Therapy, 9*(2), 1-17.

Guerney, L. F. (2003a). The history, principles, and empirical basis of filial therapy. In R. VanFleet & L. F. Guerney (Eds.), *Casebook of Filial Therapy* (pp. 1-19). Boiling Springs, PA: Play Therapy Press.

Guerney, L. F. (2003b). Filial play therapy. In C. Schaefer (Ed.), *Foundations of Play Therapy* (pp. 99-142). Hoboken, NJ: John Wiley & Sons.

Guerney, L. F. (no date). *Family Play Observations.* Unpublished paper, State College, PA.

Guerney, L. F., & Guerney, B. G., Jr. (1987). Integrating child and family therapy. *Psychotherapy, 24,* 609-614.

Guerney, L. F., & Ryan, V. M. (2013). *Group Filial Therapy: A Complete Guide to Teaching Parents to Play Therapeutically With Their Children.* London, England: Jessica Kingsley.

Harris, Z., & Landreth, G. (1995). Filial therapy with incarcerated mothers: A five week model. *International Journal of Play Therapy, 6*(2), 53-73.

Hutton, D. (2004). Filial therapy: Shifting the balance. *Clinical Child Psychology and Psychiatry, 9*(2), 261-270.

James, B. (1994). *Handbook for Treatment of Attachment-Trauma Problems in Children.* New York: The Free Press.

Jang, M. (2000). Effectiveness of filial therapy for Korean parents. *International Journal of Play Therapy, 9*(2), 39-55.

Johnson-Clark, K. (1996). The effect of filial therapy on child conduct behavior problems and the quality of the parent-child relationship. *Dissertation Abstracts International, 57*(4), 2868B.

Kale, A., & Landreth, G. (1999). Filial therapy with parents of children experiencing learning difficulties. *International Journal of Play Therapy, 8*(2), 35-56.

Landreth, G. L., & Bratton, S. C. (2006). *Child Parent Relationship Therapy (CPRT)*. New York, NY: Routledge.

Landreth, G. L., & Lobaugh, A. (1998). Filial therapy with incarcerated fathers: Effects on parental acceptance of child, parental stress, and child adjustment. *Journal of Counseling and Development, 76,* 157-165.

Lee, M. (2003). Filial therapy with immigrant Korean parents in the United States. (Doctoral dissertation, University of North Texas, 2002). *Dissertation Abstracts International, A 63*(09), 3115.

Lilly, J. P. (2003). Filial therapy to facilitate family reunification. In R. VanFleet & L. F. Guerney (Eds.), *Casebook of Filial Therapy* (pp. 185-208). Boiling Springs, PA: Play Therapy Press.

Malon, S. (2003). The efficacy of filial therapy with kinship care. In R. VanFleet & L. F. Guerney (Eds.), *Casebook of Filial Therapy* (pp. 209-234). Boiling Springs, PA: Play Therapy Press.

Mochi, C., & VanFleet, R. (2009). Roles play therapists play: Post-disaster engagement and empowerment of survivors. *Play Therapy, 4*(4), 16-18.

Oxman, L. (1972). The effectiveness of filial therapy: A controlled study. (Doctoral dissertation, Rutgers University, New Brunswick, NJ, 1971). *Dissertation Abstracts International, 32,* 6656.

Pernet, K., & Caplin, W. (in progress). *Short-Term Group Filial Therapy for Disadvantaged Families.* Oakland, CA: Growth Through Play Therapy Training Associates..

Perry, B. D., & Szalavitz, M. (2010). *Born for Love: Why Empathy is Essential--and Endangered.* New York: HarperCollins.

Ramos, A. M. M. (2003). Filial therapy after domestic violence. In R. VanFleet & L. F. Guerney (Eds.), *Casebook of Filial Therapy* (pp. 171-183). Boiling Springs, PA: Play Therapy Press.

Reynolds, C. A. (2003). Filial therapy with parents earning GEDs. In R. VanFeet & L. F. Guerney (Eds.), *Casebook of Filial Therapy* (pp. 351-359). Boiling Springs, PA: Play Therapy Press.

Ryan, V. (2004). Adapting non-directive play therapy for children with attachment disorders. *Clinical Child Psychology and Psychiatry, 9*(1), 75-87.

Ryan, V. (2007). Filial Therapy: Helping children and new carers to form secure attachment relationships. *British Journal of Social Work, 37*(4), 643-657.

Ryan, V., & Wilson, K. (1995). Non-directive play therapy as a means of recreating optimal infant socialization patterns. *Early Development and Parenting, 4*(1), 29-38.

Sensue, M. E. (1981). *Filial Therapy Follow-Up Study: Effects on Parental Acceptance and Child Adjustment.* Unpublished doctoral dissertation, The Pennsylvania State University, University Park, PA.

Smith, N. R. (2000). *A Comparative Analysis of Intensive Filial Therapy With Intensive Individual Play Therapy and Intensive Sibling Group Play Therapy With Child Witnesses of Domestic Violence.* Unpublished doctoral dissertation, University of North Texas, Denton.

Sniscak, C. C. (2003). Filial therapy with children with attention deficit hyperactivity disorder. In R. VanFleet & L. F. Guerney (Eds.), *Casebook of Filial Therapy* (pp. 85-111). Boiling Springs, PA: Play Therapy Press.

Sroufe, L. A. (1983). Infant-caregiver attachment and patterns of adaptation in the preschool: The roots of competence and maladaptation. In M. Perlmutter (Ed.), *Minnesota Symposia in Child Psychology* (Vol. 16, pp. 41-83). Hillsdale, NJ: Lawrence Erlbaum Associates.

Sroufe, L. A., & Rutter, M. (1984). The domain of developmental psychopathology. *Child Development, 55,* 17-29.

Stinnett, N., & DeFrain, J. (1985). *Secrets of Strong Families.* New York: Berkley Books.

Stover, L., & Guerney, B. G., Jr. (1967). The efficacy of training procedures for mothers in filial therapy. *Psychotherapy, 4,* 110-115.

Sullivan, H. S. (1947). *Conceptions of Modern Psychiatry.* Washington, D.C.: The William Alanson White Psychiatric Foundation.

Sweeney, D. S. (2003). Filial therapy in foster care. In R. VanFleet & L. F. Guerney (Eds.), *Casebook of Filial Therapy* (pp. 235-257). Boiling Springs, PA: Play Therapy Press.

Sywulak, A. E. (1977). *The Effect of Filial Therapy on Parental Acceptance and Child Adjustment.* Unpublished doctoral dissertation, The Pennsylvania State University, University Park, PA.

Sywulak, A. E. (2003). If the child is boss, the boss needs to be fired: Filial therapy for children with ODD. In R. VanFleet & L. F. Guerney (Eds.), *Casebook of Filial Therapy* (pp. 49-64). Boiling Springs, PA: Play Therapy Press.

Tew, K. (1997). The efficacy of filial therapy with families with chronically ill children. *Dissertation Abstracts International, 58*(3), 754A.

Topham, G. L., & VanFleet, R. (2011). Filial Therapy: A structured and straightforward approach to including young children in family therapy. *Australian and New Zealand Journal of Family Therapy, 32*(2), 144-158.

Topham, G. L., VanFleet, R., & Sniscak, C. C. (2013). Overcoming complex trauma with Filial Therapy. In C. Malchiodi and D.A. Crenshaw (Eds.), *Play and Creative Arts Therapy for Attachment Trauma.* New York: Guilford.

Topham, G. L., Wampler, K. S., Titus, G., & Rolling, E. (2011). Predicting parent and child outcomes of a filial therapy program. *International Journal of Play Therapy, 20*(2), 79-93.

VanFleet, R. (1992). Using filial therapy to strengthen families with chronically ill children. In L. VandeCreek, S. Knapp, & T. L. Jackson (Eds.), *Innovations in Clinical Practice: A Source Book* (Vol. 11, pp. 87-97). Sarasota, FL: Professional Resource Press.

VanFleet, R. (1994). Filial therapy for adoptive children and parents. In K. J. O'Connor & C. E. Schaefer (Eds.), *Handbook of Play Therapy (Vol. 2): Advances and Innovations* (pp. 371-385). New York: John Wiley & Sons.

VanFleet, R. (1997). Play and perfectionism: Putting fun back into families. In H. G. Kaduson, D. Cangelosi, & C. Schaefer (Eds.), *The Playing Cure* (pp. 61-82). Northvale, NJ: Jason Aronson.

VanFleet, R. (1999). *An Introduction to Filial Play Therapy: Video Workshop Manual.* Boiling Springs, PA: Play Therapy Press.

VanFleet, R. (2000). Short-term play therapy for families with chronic illness. In H. G. Kaduson & C. E. Schaefer (Eds.), *Short-Term Play Therapy for Children* (pp. 175-193). New York: Guilford.

VanFleet, R. (2003a). Filial therapy for adoptive children and parents. In R. VanFleet & L. F. Guerney (Eds.), *Casebook of Filial Therapy* (pp. 259-278). Boiling Springs, PA: Play Therapy Press.

VanFleet, R. (2003b). Short-term filial therapy for families with chronic illness. In R. VanFleet & L. F. Guerney (Eds.), *Casebook of Filial Therapy* (pp. 65-83). Boiling Springs, PA: Play Therapy Press.

VanFleet, R. (2004). *Filial Therapy Instructor Manual.* Boiling Springs, PA: Play Therapy Press.

VanFleet, R. (2006a). *Child-Centered Play Therapy* [DVD]. Boiling Springs, PA: Play Therapy Press.

VanFleet, R. (2006b). *Introduction to Filial Therapy* [DVD]. Boiling Springs, PA: Play Therapy Press.

VanFleet, R. (2006c). Short-term play therapy with adoptive families: Facilitating adjustment and attachment with Filial Therapy. In H.G. Kaduson and C.E. Schaefer (Eds.), *Short-Term Play Therapy for Children* (2nd ed., pp. 145-168). New York: Guilford.

VanFleet, R. (2007). *Overcoming Resistance: Engaging Parents in Play Therapy* [DVD]. Boiling Springs, PA: Play Therapy Press.

VanFleet, R. (2008). *Filial Play Therapy* [DVD] (part of Jon Carlson's DVD series on children and adolescents). Washington, D.C.: American Psychological Association.

VanFleet, R. (2009a). Filial Therapy. In K.J. O'Connor & L.D. Braverman (Eds.), *Play Therapy Theory and Practice: Comparing Theories and Techniques* (2nd ed., pp. 163-201). Hoboken, NJ: John Wiley & Sons.

VanFleet, R. (2009b). Filial Therapy: Theoretical integration, empirical validation, and practical application. In A.A. Drewes (Ed.), *Blending Play Therapy with Cognitive Behavioral Therapy* (pp. 257-279). Hoboken, NJ: John Wiley & Sons.

VanFleet, R. (2011a). Filial Therapy: What every play therapist should know (Part One). *Play Therapy: Magazine of the British Association of Play Therapists, Spring, 65,* 16-19.

VanFleet, R. (2011b). Filial Therapy: What every play therapist should know (Part Two). *Play Therapy: Magazine of the British Association of Play Therapists, Summer, 66,* 7-10.

VanFleet, R. (2011c). Filial Therapy: What every play therapist should know (Part Three). *Play Therapy: Magazine of the British Association of Play Therapists, Fall, 67,* 18-21.

VanFleet, R. (2012a). *A Parent's Handbook of Filial Therapy* (2nd ed.). Boiling Springs, PA: Play Therapy Press.

VanFleet, R. (2012b). Communication and connection: Filial Therapy with families of children with ASD. In L. Gallo-Lopez and L.C. Rubin (Eds.), *Play-Based Interventions for Children and Adolescents with Autism Spectrum Disorders* (pp. 193-208). New York: Routledge.

VanFleet, R., & Guerney, L. F. (2003). *Casebook of Filial Therapy.* Boiling Springs, PA: Play Therapy Press.

VanFleet, R., & Mochi, C. (in press). *Empowering Disaster Survivors: Application of Clinical and Community Psychology Principles and Methods for Children, Adults, Families, and Communites in a Post-Disaster Environment.* Sarasota, FL: Professional Resource Press.

VanFleet, R., Ryan, S. D., & Smith, S. (2005). A critical review of filial therapy interventions. In L. Reddy & C. E. Schaefer (Eds.), *Empirically-Based Play Interventions for Children.* Washington, D.C.: American Psychological Association.

VanFleet, R., & Sniscak, C. C. (2003a). Filial therapy for attachment-disrupted and disordered children. In R. VanFleet & L. F. Guerney (Eds.), *Casebook of Filial Therapy* (pp. 279-308). Boiling Springs, PA: Play Therapy Press.

VanFleet, R., & Sniscak, C. C. (2003b). Filial therapy for children exposed to traumatic events. In R. VanFleet & L. F. Guerney (Eds.), *Casebook of Filial Therapy* (pp. 113-137). Boiling Springs, PA: Play Therapy Press.

VanFleet, R., Sniscak, C.C., & Faa-Thompson, T. (2013). *Filial Therapy Groups for Foster and Adoptive Parents: Building Attachment in a 14 to 18 Week Family Program.* Boiling Springs, PA: Play Therapy Press.

VanFleet, R., Sywulak, A. E., & Sniscak, C. C. (2010). *Child-Centered Play Therapy.* New York: Guilford.

VanFleet, R., & Topham, G. (2011). Filial Therapy for maltreated and neglected children: Integration of family therapy and play therapy. In A. Drewes, S.C. Bratton, & C.E. Schaefer (Eds.), *Integrative Play Therapy* (pp. 153-175). Hoboken, NJ: John Wiley & Sons.

Wallerstein, J. S., & Blakeslee, S. (1989). *Second Chances: Men, Women & Children a Decade After Divorce.* New York: Ticknor & Fields.

Wallerstein, J. S., & Kelly, J. B. (1980). *Surviving the Breakup: How Children and Parents Cope With Divorce.* New York: Basic Books.

White, J., Draper, K., & Flynt, M. (2003). Kinder training: A school counselor and teacher consultation model integrating filial therapy and Adlerian theory. In R. VanFleet & L. F. Guerney (Eds.), *Casebook of Filial Therapy* (pp. 331-350). Boiling Springs, PA: Play Therapy Press.

Wright, C., & Walker, J. (2003). Using filial therapy with Head Start families. In R. VanFleet & L. F. Guerney (Eds.), *Casebook of Filial Therapy* (pp. 309-329). Boiling Springs, PA: Play Therapy Press.